DIANA
Living Through Life's Challenges

A Courageous Overcoming Through Love

By

Miri Arlen
and
Diana The Calico Cat

Photography by Wayne Allen

© 2003 by Miriam Erb Allen. All rights reserved.

No part of this book may be reproduced, stored in a retrieval system, or transmitted by any means, electronic, mechanical, photocopying, recording, or otherwise, without written permission from the author.

ISBN: 1-4033-4125-7 (e-book)
ISBN: 1-4033-4126-5 (Paperback)

This book is printed on acid free paper.

Photography Copyright © 2002 by Wayne Allen

1stBooks - rev. 1/23/03

To Wayne:

Your sharing, support and example
Have helped me more than anyone or
Anything else to realize that I can
Accept change and limitation
And
Continue to enjoy life!

—Diana

Without your loving support
At all stages of its development,
This book would never
Have been born.
Thank you!

—Miri

You must be willing to let go of trying to make things happen the way you want them to and think they should, and just be present with whatever is there and accept it as it is.

—Diana

Diana's pawprint

CONTENTS

Acknowledgements ix

Foreword: Maurice Friedman xi

Preface xiii

Miri's Introduction: How This Book Came To Be xvii

Part A: DIANA'S STORY

Diana's Introduction 3

Chapter 1:   My Friend Jason 9

Chapter 2:   I Get Very Sick 19

Chapter 3:   Shots And Energy Swings 27

Chapter 4:   Hunting, My Yard, And Other Joys 35

Chapter 5:   A Stranger Hunts In My Yard 45

Chapter 6:   My Life Goes On 53

Chapter 7:   Jada Arrives 61

Chapter 8:   Reflections 73

Part B: MIRI'S STORY

Chapter 9:   Learning To Hear Diana 85

Chapter 10:   Working With Diana On Her Book 93

Chapter 11:   Remembering Diana 99

Epilogue: Life Continues to Unfold 109

Major Events In Diana's Life 113
Related Reading 115
About The Authors 119
About the Book and Diana 121

ACKNOWLEDGEMENTS:

Without the support, inspiration and guidance of **Spirit** throughout every step of the way, this book would never have come into being. There are also two people without whom this book would not exist: **Samantha Khury,** professional interspecies communicator, and my beloved husband, **Wayne.**

Through her work with our cat companions, Diana and Jason, **Samantha** showed me that human-animal dialogue really can take place. She also inspired the idea of this book while discussing with Diana what might help give her meaning and help her feel useful during the slow recovery from her illness and leg injury.

Wayne spent what must have totaled at least hundreds of hours, through three computer crashes and numerous other mechanical and electrical malfunctions, helping me continue to have to have a working computer. He also photographed, scanned, and edited most of the images for the book. Wayne supported and encouraged me through low points of stuckness and celebrated with me my breakthroughs and progress. His suggestions and feedback were invaluable.

Our dear cat companion, **Jada,** supported me with her energy and love through periods of focus on the book, even though she would have liked more of my attention to center on her.

Trusted friend and colleague, Dr. **Mel Karmen,** gave me feedback and validation at all stages of the book's development. Mel was available to my clients when I focused on writing, and he also supported us through his editorial assistance and words of endorsement of the book.

Drs. **Maurice** and **Aleene Friedman** were willing to "suspend disbelief", and reviewed and critiqued an early draft of the book. I am grateful for their helpful suggestions and encouragement to continue, and to Maurice for his support through writing a forward for the book.

Stephen Blake, D.V.M., helped save Diana's life on at least two occasions through his fine, dedicated medical care, for which I will be eternally grateful. I also appreciate his words of endorsement of Diana.

Thanks to the excellent, devoted medical care of **Anne Smith,** V.M.D., Diana and I had another six months together after her kidney failure. Dr. Smith also encouraged me to complete the book and supported it through her words of endorsement.

Sue Goodrich, professional animal consultant, helped Diana and Jada become more accepting of their differences. She also supported Diana and me through the last few years of Diana's life (after Samantha no longer came to San Diego), and validated our work through her words of endorsement of the book.

Stephanie Follas helped us immeasurably in the return of Jason as Jada. She also reviewed an early draft of the book and gave a number of helpful suggestions.

Kathleen Estabrook, gave useful suggestions after reviewing the last draft of the book, and also wrote words of support for the book.

Dr. **Cynthia Harris** reviewed and gave helpful feedback to an early draft and supported my continuing to move ahead with the book.

Dr. **Jean Campbell,** Dr. **Barbara Muriello,** and **Dean Doss** all gave helpful suggestions at various stages of the book's progress, and encouraged us to keep on keeping on.

Members of a creative non-fiction writing class taught by **Judith Barkley,** especially **Emily Jorgensen** and **Mickey Mikalauskas**, gave me supportive and constructive critique of the first several chapters of the book. The feedback of **Patty**, member of a writing group I was briefly part of, was also deeply appreciated.

The critique and suggestions of **Judy Reeves**, professional writer, helped me fine-tune a later draft of the book.

The sensitive, intuitive, hypnotic work of **Stephen Gilligan**, Ph.D., assisted me in moving through my blocks and more fully trusting my heart and my own inner guidance.

I am deeply thankful for the support and encouragement of my children and for the openness of some of my family of origin to consider the possibility of interspecies communication, even though this idea is foreign to their belief system.

I am also very grateful to my parents for their love, for their support of my connection to animals as a child, and for their acceptance of my taking a different life path than they would have chosen for me.

FOREWORD

Miri Arlen's beautiful book about her cat Diana is the most unusual piece of literature that I have ever encountered. It goes beyond May Sarton's lovely cat-novel *The Fur Person*, for it is not a book *about* Diana but *by* Diana.

The story is told by Diana herself; through Miri, to be sure, but definitely not in the third person. It is a first person communication that takes us well beyond Coleridge's "willing suspension of disbelief" into a world in which only meditation, simplicity, and clearing the mind can enable Miri (and through her, us) to hear what Diana is trying to tell her. Once one has got over this hurdle, a lovely, heart-warming, and yes, heart-wrenching setting unfolds before us that forcefully conveys Diana's desire to help children who have diabetes to live with the insulin shots and the other disturbances and indignities that are necessary for the diabetic person—cat or human—to stay alive.

One feels Miri in the immediate background, of course, and Wayne, himself a diabetic, in the somewhat farther removed background.

But above all it is Diana's tale. Through pictures and narratives, Diana becomes fully present to us in all the complexity of her feline world. Diana's friendship with Jason and later with Jada—the kitten whom Miri believes is Jason's reincarnation—are as vivid as the brutal attack of the fox who wants to kill and eat Diana just as she kills and eats the small "critters" that come under her ever-watchful huntress gaze.

We readers are carried along with the bittersweet current that buoys up Diana's life. Children and adults alike will find Diana's story vivid and totally engrossing as she tells it through Miri.

Maurice Friedman, Ph.D.

Professor Emeritus of Religious Studies,
  Philosophy, and Comparative Literature
San Diego State University

Author of: *Touchstones of Reality,*
  Encounter on the Narrow Ridge: A Life of Martin Buber, and
  The Affirming Flame: A Poetics of Meaning.

PREFACE

This is a book about love, about the difference a deep bond of love made in the life of a cat and of a human. My relationship with Diana has shown me the depth of love possible with another species, just as my relationship with Wayne, my husband, has shown me the depth of love that is possible with another human.

This book is also the story of a wise, beautiful, and strong-willed calico cat, Diana, and of her human, Miri, as she learns to communicate with her. Diana struggled deeply with existential questions after her best friend, Jason, died and she faced a life-threatening health crisis herself. She wanted to share with others what helped her be able to cope with these life challenges and continue to live with joy and meaning in spite of them.

As I worked with Diana on this book, I was amazed again and again by the depth of her perception and awareness and by the courage and honesty with which she faced the changes she had to make. She showed me clearly that cats are spiritual beings, and have awareness and abilities that many of us humans have lost or never developed.

I always felt a deep bond of connection with the animals I grew up with on a farm, and I often had a sense of what they were thinking and feeling. But when I first heard about interspecies telepathic communicators, I initially felt quite skeptical (though also curious) about the possibility that animals could communicate more specific thoughts, feelings, and information in a way a human would be able to "hear."

This all changed when Samantha Khury, a professional interspecies telepathic communicator, shared with my husband Wayne and me what our cat companions had shared with her. We could no longer doubt that two-way communication had occurred between our cats and Samantha because of the validity of the many things Samantha reported to us that she could not have known in any other way.

I had to write this book with Diana for my own soul's development. It is not something I decided rationally that I wanted to do; in fact, I initially did not want to do it. Working on this book has made me face and work through deep inner fears and negativity in order to be able to move ahead. I tried to back out of the task a number of times, but it would not let me go. The result is in your hands.

I want you to know that if I could learn to "hear" my animal companions, despite all of my questioning and disbelief, you can too, if you truly want to do so.

Miri

DIANA
Living Through Life's Challenges

A Courageous Overcoming Through Love

Miri and Diana

Miri's Introduction:

HOW THIS BOOK CAME TO BE

"Go back and write the book with Diana."
"*What?*" With disbelief I heard the message repeated.
"Go back and write the book with Diana!"
"*Me, Great One? I don't know how to do this.*"
"You can learn to do so."
"*How can I possibly do this? I don't have the gift of communicating with animals. I don't know how to write a book.*"
"Just go back and start. Spend more time alone with Diana, ask her questions, and be open to "hearing" whatever she wants to share with you. The way to move ahead will open as you go and do this. Diana needs you to connect with her in this way, and you need to be open to receiving from her."

What I was being told to do seemed very clear. Somehow, learning to hear Diana and write the book with her appeared to be the next step on my own soul's journey, in ways I did not begin to understand. The task felt very huge and sacred, and I felt totally unprepared, unworthy, and afraid.

In the midst of a crisis of personal meaning, I had gone alone to the quiet of the desert for several days to meditate, and pray for guidance and direction. But this was not what I expected or wanted to hear. It did not fit with my image of myself as a psychologist and rational person. Something about it was very deeply unsettling, and in some vague way, it even felt dangerous.

I grew up on a farm, and I've always felt a deep love for and close connection to animals. It was painful for me when steers, lambs, and turkeys I'd grown to love were butchered or sold, all routine occurrences on a farm. At around age eleven I became a vegetarian for several years after a duck friend was killed and eaten for dinner.

As a child, I often felt like I knew what my animal friends were feeling or wanting. This was a general kind of awareness, often with behavioral cues. I'd never thought seriously about the possibility of animals actually sharing specific thoughts or factual information with humans. As I grew up and was taught to be more "reasonable," much of this childhood sense of knowing also faded from my consciousness.

In recent years, I'd profoundly experienced the reality of human-animal communication through the work of Samantha Khury, a professional interspecies communication therapist, with our cat companions, Diana and Jason. I'd heard about Samantha through a friend, who'd told me that Samantha had met with her pets and helped them resolve some problem behaviors. My friend said that her cat who had frequently peed on the floor stopped doing so after meeting with Samantha.

Skeptical but curious, my husband Wayne and I made an appointment for Diana and Jason (and ourselves!) to meet with Samantha. We both had scientific training in our backgrounds, and the idea of a human communicating with animals in a way that included clearly hearing specific details and information from the animals' thoughts and feelings went against all we'd been taught. Such things were considered anthropomorphizing at best. But, in spite of this, we felt open to expanding our awareness, depending on what happened as a result of the meeting with Samantha.

At our initial meeting with Samantha, we asked for help with three problem areas:

Miri's Introduction

(1) Diana frequently brought her prey into the house and ate them there. This often resulted in bloodstains on our carpet and maggots crawling from the dried blood if we hadn't noticed and cleaned up the dried blood soon enough. We wanted Diana to kill and eat her prey outside.

(2) Jason became upset when Wayne and I petted Diana and tried to push his way in between her and us, even if he was getting as much attention as she. Diana, in deference to Jason, usually withdrew and stayed in the background when Jason was around. We desired to be able to give them more equal attention without this upsetting Jason.

(3) Jason clawed our living room furniture badly, especially one orange upholstered chair. We wanted him to use a scratching post to sharpen his claws.

Samantha first listened carefully to our concerns and then met alone with Diana and Jason for about an hour. Following her time alone with them, she shared with us what they had told her in response to her questions and what she had discussed with them.

Diana explained to Samantha that she'd started bringing me prey and other presents because she wanted to do her part and help out when she'd realized I was having a hard time making ends meet. Samantha then explained to Diana why we wanted her to eat her prey outside and asked her to please do so. In keeping with this request, she also gave Diana the task of patrolling the boundaries of the house and not allowing any other animals to come inside.

Jason, Samantha said, saw himself as our baby boy and felt like he needed and owned us. She affirmed his belief that he was in fact our baby boy, but added that Diana was also our baby girl. She explained to him that we loved Diana as well as him and that we had enough love for them both.

Jason then described to Samantha how much he enjoyed deeply sinking his claws into the soft upholstered furniture! Only very reluctantly did he agree to use a scratching post *if* we put one in a central place in the living room. He was not willing to have to go to a back room and use the scratching post that was there.

Diana Living Through Life's Challenges

There was definite improvement in all of our three areas of concern after the meeting with Samantha, shown as follows:

(1) For the next several months Diana killed and ate her prey outside, as requested. When she briefly started bringing prey into the house again, she immediately improved when reminded by our both telling her and carrying her and her prey outside if we caught her with a critter in the house.
(2) Jason became more accepting of our noticing and petting Diana as long as he was receiving attention when she was. Diana also became more accepting of our giving her attention and petting, although she still gave some deference to Jason as first cat.
(3) When we put a scratching post in the living room as Jason requested, he used the post and stopped clawing the living room furniture except when he was very mad at us.

We were impressed by these changes in Diana and Jason's behavior. Whatever Samantha did when she was with them clearly made a difference. In subsequent sessions, Samantha helped all of us find our way through the difficult times of Jason's illness and death and Diana's illness and serious injury to her leg.

After the fox hurt her leg, Diana described her attacker to Samantha as having a long, thin face, a bushy tail, and as being gray with some darker markings. Her description occurred before we had any idea that a fox was coming into our "well-fenced" (we thought) yard, and we were puzzled as to what animal it could be. The face sounded like an opossum but the tail didn't.

There was a mean cat in the neighborhood who had a bushy tail, but his face wasn't long and thin and he wasn't gray. We lived along an extremely busy street, and hadn't even considered that it might be a fox, until I caught it in a trap after Diana was injured a second time. The fox fit Diana's previous description exactly.

Jason, in a later session, told Samantha how afraid he still was of getting lost and hurt since a traumatic experience he'd had as a kitten. He'd slipped out of a car door, nearly gotten run over as he ran in terror across a busy street, and had no idea where he was. He said that

Miri's Introduction

he continued to be afraid of getting lost because of this experience and that was why he so intensely hated being in cars.

I had been present during the traumatic experience Jason described and I had not told Samantha about it.

Samantha was clearly an expert at what she did. Convinced of the validity of her work by the results she obtained, we were grateful for her loving and compassionate assistance.

The idea of Diana's book was conceived during a session Diana had with Samantha after her leg had been injured and was healing very slowly because of her diabetes, and it reappeared in all subsequent sessions. Samantha felt that working on a book to share her experiences with others would be an excellent way for Diana to again become meaningfully involved in life while having to spend most of her time lying around recovering.

Very disheartened at the time, Diana liked the idea that she could potentially help children going through similar experiences by sharing about what had helped her cope with and transcend the changes and limitations caused by her serious illness and injury.

Samantha was originally willing to work with Diana on her book, but became ill and was not able to do so after all. Samantha suggested that I spend more time with Diana and start working on the book with her, but at the time I didn't consider myself capable of doing this. I waited...and waited some more, hoping Samantha would soon become well enough to take on this task.

It gradually became apparent that Samantha would not be able to work with Diana on the book in the near future. It was clear that Diana greatly needed something to help her know she still had something to contribute as well as to again feel special in the face of young Jada's arrival and attempted takeover of our home and attention. I loved Diana very deeply. And there was no questioning what I had been told to do while in the desert asking for direction and guidance.

Could I possibly do what was being asked of me? My instructions were to begin by spending more time with Diana, asking her questions, and being open to whatever I might receive from her in response. The task sounded so deceptively simple.

Diana Living Through Life's Challenges

I felt like I had no real choice but to give this task my best, for love of Diana and of myself. The saga of my journey learning to hear Diana follows her story in Part B of the book.

I now turn you over to Diana as she tells her story through me as best I understood it.

Part A: DIANA'S STORY

Diana in her favorite box

DIANA'S INTRODUCTION

I am an elderly cat who has lived through many challenging experiences. I want to tell you my story, hoping it will help you have the courage to keep going on through hard times in your life. I hope my sharing will help you know you can continue to love, play, and experience life deeply, even when you are sick, hurt, have lost a dear friend, or have to make unexpected life changes.

I would also like to expand your understanding of what it's like to be a cat by sharing some of my thoughts, feelings, joys, sorrows and insights. I hope you'll learn from and enjoy my story!

I've lived with Miri, my human mom, ever since she took me home from an animal shelter when I was a baby. Miri named me Diana after a goddess of hunting. I lived up to my name and became an excellent huntress! Jason ("Jase"), a gentle, large, tan, snuggly cat, was my best friend from the time I first came home with Miri until he got sick and died several years ago. Wayne, a big strong man with a sensitive musical soul, has also been an important member of my family ever since Jase, Miri, and I moved to live with him many long years ago.

Diana Living Through Life's Challenges

Even though I'd experienced abandonment as a tiny baby when my mother disappeared, I came to take the goodness of my life for granted after Miri adopted me...until Jase died. I became very depressed after losing him. Then, the spring after Jase's death, I got sick with diabetes and nearly died. For a while it was hard to imagine going on living because I felt so weak and miserable.

What most helped me accept the changes and limitations that at first felt too big to deal with was knowing I was loved, needed and wanted even though I couldn't do many of the things I used to be able to do. It also helped to realize that I can choose to focus on those activities and experiences I *can* still do and enjoy rather than on what I can't do anymore. Making such positive choices helped me both feel better and again find a sense of meaning in my life.

I've had much goodness and fun in my life. As a kitten, I loved teasing Jase and then running into my cardboard box house.

Diana as a kitten

Jase couldn't catch me in my house because the doors were just big enough for me to fit through. I enjoyed seeing how fast I could run, how far I could leap, how high I could climb, and how fiercely I could pounce on Jase or on Miri's hands and feet when she moved them under a wooly blanket.

I especially liked to bat around a little plastic ball that had a bell inside. I often did this at night, and sometimes the ringing bell woke Miri up. Then she grumbled at me and hid my ball until she got up in the morning.

When I grew big enough to jump up to the window sill and go outside by myself, I had lots of good times climbing trees, pouncing on leaves, sticks and bugs, and chasing mice, rats, lizards and birds until I became fast enough to catch them.

Diana as a teenager

I loved to explore the area around my home, check out what was happening, and watch all the different things animals and people did and how the plants, weather, and seasons changed. I learned how fast I needed to run and/or how far I needed to leap to catch a mouse or bird and how hard I needed to bat my plastic ball to make it go where I wanted it to.

I often teased two big tough neighbor dogs by walking along a tree branch that hung over their yard. When they weren't too close, I sometimes jumped down into their yard. Then they ran after me, barking furiously, thinking they could catch me. How foolish they were! I knew I was much faster than they were for short distances.

After we moved to live with Wayne, I enjoyed teasing a little shaggy white dog from the top of the garage roof between our yards. He smelled me and searched all over his yard for me, but his long hair covered his eyes and he never saw me up on the roof.

It was good to know I was really fast and strong, and that I could protect myself, Jase, and my yard. It was good to have a home to come back to where I was warm, fed, and cared about. I felt loved and special when Miri admired, petted, and talked to me and when Wayne "sweet-talked" me as only he could do. I felt very loved, too, when Jase licked my face, played with me, and when I curled up next to his warm, furry body as we rested during the day. All four of us slept snuggled next to each other at night.

I always did my best to contribute whatever I could to my family, especially when Miri was having a hard time making ends meet. I couldn't go out and get a job that paid money, so I brought things home to Miri that I thought she'd like and be able to use.
Miri made shelves and cabinets out of wood back then, so I brought her a metal tape measure I saw someone using to work with wood. It was kind of heavy, and she was very impressed when I carried it home. She said we should maybe give it back to whomever I took it from, but she ended up keeping and treasuring it as a present from me.

Since Miri didn't like to eat freshly killed critters, I tried to find pieces of food I thought she might like. I wasn't too successful at that. Miri smoked then, so I brought her half-packs of cigarettes whenever I found any lying around, even though I didn't like the smoke. She always thanked me for everything I brought her. It gave me great joy to help and please Miri in any way I could.
After we moved to be with Wayne, I got the task of keeping mice and rats under control in the woodpiles and shed area. This job was fun, as I always enjoyed catching and eating critters, and it made Wayne and Miri happy, so that made me happy, too.

As you can see, my early life after Miri adopted me was carefree and full of goodness. Until Jase died, I thought it would always be

Diana's Introduction

that way. Go back in time with me now as I remember some of my important life experiences, what helped me through difficult times, and what gave and gives me joy and meaning.

Jason

Chapter 1

MY FRIEND JASON

    Jason (Jase) was the most wonderful friend, playmate, and companion anyone could ever have. When I was a small kitten, he licked my face and washed me all over with his big rough tongue. He allowed me to jump on him, "attack" him fiercely, and even pounce on his tail, though he didn't like that very much.

    Jase watched over me to make sure I was okay, especially when I grew big enough to jump up onto the window ledge and go outside through the small cat "door" under the window. He didn't feel safe going outside our yard, though, so I was on my own when I left our yard to explore the neighborhood.

    When I began catching mice and other critters, Jase praised me even though he wasn't very good at catching anything himself, not even a fly. He sometimes gave me an intense stern look if I teased him too much when he wanted to be quiet. If I kept on after his look, he would swat me hard. But mostly Jase was patient, accepting, and playful with me. And he was *always* there for me whenever I needed him. It just isn't the same since he's gone.

Jase and I would lie for hours with our heads, legs, or backs touching or snuggled tightly together. If I lay my head on his side I could feel and hear the rhythm of his heartbeat. I loved the soft, warm, comforting feeling of his body next to mine. I guess he took the place of my mother and sister in that way.

Baby Diana and Jase

Jase also liked to lie next to Miri and Wayne at night, and didn't want me to lie too close to them when he was there. Though I would have liked to also lie next to them, I understood that Jase needed to feel special in this way. I could accept Jase lying closer in to Miri and Wayne because I knew they loved me and because he gave me so much love, too.

As I grew older, Jase and I continued to often snuggle close together as we rested, with some part of our bodies in touch. I continued to love the feeling of his soft fur and the warmth and comfort of his body next to mine, as long as we were together.

My Friend Jason

Diana and Jase lying close together.

Jase was top cat in the house with Miri and Wayne. He never tried to take my food, though. Maybe he knew that would have been too much for me to handle. Food becomes pretty important when you've nearly starved to death as a baby.

But out in my yard I've always been top cat. Jase was easily frightened outside because he was lost and nearly got run over by a car when he was a baby. He was afraid to be out of the house alone, even in our fenced-in yard. Whenever he came out, I made sure no other animals were around and let him know it was safe. I mostly stayed nearby watching out for him, especially as he got older and didn't feel well.

I've delighted in being outside from the day I first went there on my own; the sunshine, the breeze, and the trees, bushes, flowers, birds, butterflies, bees, mice, rats, lizards and other critters all around! But special as being outdoors has always been for me, I also loved being with Jase. So I divided my time between being outside and being with him as best I could, even though I much preferred being out in my yard.

I thought more sunshine and fresh air would be good for Jase, and tried to get him to come out in the sun and play more. He often came out for a while to please me, though I think he enjoyed it as long as I was with him. I did anything I could to help him feel safe. We were so close that I felt unhappy too if Jase was unhappy and safe and good if he felt safe and happy.

Touching Heads

I loved to just be near Jase, to look at him, smell him, hear him, and feel him next to me. His fur was a very beautiful light tan color with darker markings on his face, legs, ears, and tail. I greatly admired his most magnificent, fluffy, striped tail, as mine isn't fluffy. My tail has a white tip on the end of it, though, and that's special, too. Miri and Wayne call it my flag.

Jase had dark pointed tufts on his ears and beautiful big blue eyes. He would look directly into my eyes, as though he were looking right into my soul. Sometimes we just gazed deeply into each other's eyes for a long, long time, getting lost in each other. His voice was quite loud and raspy. As he talked out loud a lot, I always knew when he was around.

My Friend Jason

Jase

Watching Jase become weak and sick as he got older was really hard for me. He stopped playing with me and wouldn't even give me that stern look of his when I teased him too much. He hardly ate anything, and often got sick in his stomach and couldn't keep food down. His horrible hacking cough continued to get worse in spite of going to the doctor many times. He gradually became thinner and weaker, until he just lay around most of the time. He was much too still, and that worried me a lot.

I brought Jase freshly killed mice and birds, hoping they would spark his interest in eating more and help him feel stronger, but he was no longer interested in food. He seemed comforted by my staying nearby, licking him, and snuggling in close. So I did those things for him and watched over him during most of our last days together. It was so very hard to feel like there was nothing I could do to stop Jase from slowly fading away from me.

Diana watching over Jase.

I remember the evening Jase left us so clearly, as though it just happened. Some friends are gathered with Miri and Dr. Blake to help send him on his journey with love. They invite me to join them, but I can't stand the thought of watching Jase "die." I'm not sure exactly what dying means, but it feels very bad, like he'll be gone forever. I can't imagine being without him.

Jase has been the sweetness in my life, as long as I can remember. Oh, he has had his moments, like getting jealous when Miri and Wayne give me attention. But he's **always** been there to lie next to, wash my face, tease and play with, or, since he's been so sick, to watch over, care for, protect, and comfort.

My heart is crying out: *"Jase, please don't leave me! I need you! I love you so very much. I know you haven't been feeling well, and I'll catch you more fresh critters to help you feel better again. I'll stay by your side **all** the time. Please don't leave me."* My heart feels about to break at the thought.

My Friend Jason

Jase is gone. Miri is crying. I want to scream out, but the sounds are stuck in my throat. Miri asks me if I want to go over to Jase's body and say goodbye, but I don't want to do that. I don't want to be closer to his body if he's not there. I don't want him to be gone. I just want to hide away somewhere by myself. It feels like a big hole has been ripped out of the middle of my heart and part of me is missing.

Jase's body is so still; he isn't in it anymore. I can't believe he's really left me. I can't imagine being able to go on living without him here with me.

I don't understand how Miri and Dr. Blake could help make Jase leave his body and be gone from us just because he was sick. Didn't Miri want him here anymore? What if I get sick? Will she then not want me here, too?

I feel alone, helpless, and abandoned again, like I felt long ago when my mother was suddenly gone. Miri reaches out, trying to comfort me, but I pull away from her. She senses how badly I feel and would like to help me feel better. I know she loves me, but she can't make up for Jase.

Besides, Miri's about to go somewhere far away to visit her family. I thought Jase would always be here with me, but now he's gone, and Miri's going away, too. Wayne has already left.

Miri tells me someone will be staying here with me all the time she is gone, but I need **her** here right now. She and Wayne are all the family I have left. She wouldn't want to be alone right now, so how can she leave me? This isn't fair at all. I don't know what to do. I don't feel like hunting or even like being out in my yard. I just want to be very still and not do or feel anything.

When Miri first took me home from the cat shelter as a baby, Jase was there and he'd been there with me ever since. I had a home, food, warmth, and the love of Jase and Miri. I came to trust that both of them would be there for me. When we moved to live with Wayne, I learned to also trust him and to enjoy his sweet way of talking to me and telling me how beautiful and special I am. There was so much love and goodness among us all.

There's an immense sadness in my heart and a feeling of emptiness in my life now that Jase is gone. I keep expecting to see him around again, as always. Sometimes I think I do see him, but then when I look more closely I realize he isn't really there, at least not in his body. The spark is gone from my life, and it's hard for me to get involved in anything. I miss him so much!

I miss the warmth and comfort of lying next to Jase. I miss his loud raspy voice, his stern look when he's upset with me, his special Jase smell. I miss the feeling of his rough tongue washing my face and body. I miss looking deeply into his big blue eyes and having him gaze back into mine.

Nothing else can fill the huge hole that was ripped out of my heart when Jase left. It just aches whenever I think of him.

I don't feel like hunting for a long time after Jase's death. Food still provides comfort for me sometimes. It's also good to be able to snuggle in freely next to Miri and Wayne at night without Jase getting jealous of my being there. I realize how much I missed out on the goodness of their love because I always deferred to his wanting to be closer to them.

It helps me feel a little better to know that Miri needs me to be there for her. At least someone needs me.

Even though I don't feel like doing much of anything for a while, I start to distract myself by going outside and looking for critters, watching the sunshine shimmering through the trees, or watching butterflies dancing on the flowers. Doing these things takes my thoughts away from missing Jase, and the pain in my heart slowly begins to ease.

When I allow myself to get caught up in the joy and beauty of all the wonders of life and nature right here in my yard, my heart, body and spirit gradually improve. I even begin hunting again. Over time my spirit continues to heal, and I start to regain a sense of well-being and goodness in my life.

My Friend Jason

Until I get sick.

A very sick Diana in Miri's arms

Chapter 2

I GET VERY SICK

I've always been a strong and healthy cat in the past, but now I lie beside my water bowl, too weak to stand. I drift in and out of consciousness and don't know what to do.

Miri seemed quite concerned about me when I didn't eat anything this morning, but went on to work anyway. I wish she hadn't gone. Wayne is gone, too. I hope one of them will be home soon. I'm so thirsty all the time. I keep drinking more and more, but can't seem to drink enough to not feel thirsty, and then I have to pee all the time.

My awareness comes and goes as I lie here totally exhausted, waiting for someone to come and help me. I'm not able to do anything more for myself. I feel like I'm starving to death and try to eat, but am too weak to swallow food. I hardly have the strength to even drink anymore.

Before this I've mostly felt in charge of my life, able to come and go as I please. I've known what it's like to be afraid and powerless; I felt these things when Jase died and when my mother disappeared.

But those times, though very difficult, were nothing compared to the total helplessness I feel now.

I don't understand what's happening to me. I've never been so sick before. Does this mean I will die, like my friend Jase? Will Miri get Dr. Blake to come here and help me die, like she did with Jase? I'm scared!

I'm about to black out again. Maybe I'll just let myself go and not try to come back the next time I lose consciousness. But I can't do that to Miri. I remember how terribly sad I was when Jase died, and I don't want to make her feel like I did. Maybe she can do something when she sees how sick and weak I am. I hope she will take me to see Dr. Blake. He's always helped me feel better when I've been sick before. I have to hang on until Miri gets here. I love her and don't want to be parted from her, too. She and Wayne are the only family I have left.

It's strange to be on the edge of life and death, feeling like I could go either way. I'm not ready to leave Miri, but I don't have enough strength to hang on much longer. I hope she gets here soon.

Miri's finally here! I feel her warm arms around me, comforting and protecting me. I feel her loving energy flowing into my body, strengthening me and pulling me back towards life. She is pleading with me now: *"Please hang on a little longer, Diana. Please don't leave me. I can't imagine being without you. Please stay here with us, Diana."*

Miri gently cradles me in her arms, supporting my fragile connection to life until we can go see Dr. Blake. She holds me securely as Wayne drives us to Dr. Blake's office. The journey is a hazy blur as I continue hovering on the edge of awareness.

Dr. Blake says things like "critical condition", "blood sugar out of control," and "diabetic crisis" as he examines me. I'm glad Miri stays right by my side as I lie, half-conscious, an i.v. needle in one of my front legs. Other sharp needles are jabbed repeatedly into my back and other legs to take my blood and give me medicine. After a time that seems like forever, I finally drift asleep to the touch of Miri's

I Get Very Sick

hand slowly stroking my head and the sound of her voice telling me "You are going to be okay, Diana".

When I next awaken, I feel more alert. I'm also angry about the needle still stuck in my body. I struggle and bite at the needle, but am not strong enough to get it out. Miri tells me to please let it in…that I need the fluid it is giving me right now. My body feels so heavy and clumsy I can barely move a muscle.

I'm quite hungry, and am glad when Dr. Blake puts a piece of chicken in my mouth. It tastes good, and I'm able to swallow several pieces. Miri keeps telling me over and over that I am going to get better, but that I must be still and rest now because I am very sick. I don't like being so weak and I don't like the needle in my leg, but I finally stop trying to move and just let myself be soothed and calmed by Miri's caresses and soft words.

Dr. Blake explains to Miri that my body wasn't making enough insulin to digest my food and had started to consume itself. He said I was blacking out because my blood sugar had gone dangerously high. I don't fully understand what all that means, but I do know I've lost a lot of weight the past few weeks, I feel all shivery, and nothing in my body is working right. I just want to sleep…and sleep some more.

Because of how sick I am, Dr. Blake sends us to see Dr. Slusser, who knows more about diabetes than he does. I have to stay in a hospital for several days and nights under Dr. Slusser's care. Miri isn't allowed to stay with me overnight in the hospital. That's very upsetting for me. Being left alone at night in a strange place makes me feel afraid I'll be abandoned again like happened back when I was a baby and my mother disappeared.

I never saw my mother again and I have no idea what happened to her. My sweet sister and I cried and cried for her, but she never came back. We snuggled together to give each other warmth and comfort, but weren't able to feed or protect ourselves. Cold and terrified, we didn't know what would happen to us. We got so hungry we were afraid we'd starve.

A kind lady found my sister and me and fed us warm milk from a dropper because we weren't big enough to drink it from a bowl. After caring for us several days, she took us to a shelter for cats with no homes. I was in a cage just inside the front door of the cat shelter when Miri and I first saw each other. She was talking to a lady and kept looking over at me again and again. I gazed back into her brown eyes, hoping she'd take me home with her.

The shelter lady took me out of the cage and handed me to Miri. At first Miri protested and tried to hand me back, saying she wasn't ready to have another kitten. But then she held and stroked me and I fell asleep in her lap. She took me along home, and I've been with her ever since.

As I lie here alone at night looking out through the bars of my hospital cage, I feel scared and helpless again like I felt back then as a tiny baby. I want to cry, but tears won't come. It helps a little to remember that someone found and cared for me when I was abandoned as a baby. It also helps to remember that Miri told me that I will soon feel better again. She's never lied to me.

My leg is throbbing with pain where a needle is stuck into it. I bite at the needle and rub against the side of the cage, trying to get it out. I almost succeed at this, but a stern woman in a white jacket notices what I'm doing. She scolds me and calls a young man over to help.

Holding me firmly, the stern woman and young man stick a huge new needle into my throat. Then they fasten the needle to a thick collar around my neck so securely there's no way I can get it out. I'm mad but too weak to fight. At least my leg isn't throbbing anymore. It helps a little to imagine biting and scratching them so hard they scream out loudly in pain.

The heating pad I'm lying on is slowly warming up my body. It feels good, as I was quite cold. I overhear Dr. Slusser saying I'm still in critical condition. He's trying to find the right amount of insulin to bring my blood sugar to a better level and help keep it there. He says that must happen before I can go home.

I somehow make it through the long gray nights alone, knowing Miri or Wayne will come and be with me again in the morning. Dr. Slusser allows one of them to stay with me during the day while he's here. I'm very grateful to him, as I feel much safer and calmer when one of them is with me.

I miss my home awfully much as I lie in my cage in this strange place. I miss my favorite big comfortable stuffed chair to lie on. I miss the two big trees that spread like umbrellas over my yard, the blue flowered rambling bushes along the fence, and all the birds, butterflies, mice, rats and possums. I even miss the skunks! And I miss snuggling next to Miri and Wayne at night.

Diana on her favorite orange chair

My imagination is so good I can almost feel the soft plush seat of my chair, the moist coolness of the earth, and the warmth of the sun on my back. But even my excellent imagining is not nearly as good as really being there. It wouldn't be so hard to be sick if I could at least be resting in my favorite familiar places.

I just heard Dr. Slusser telling Miri I can go home! That is *so* good to hear! I've been feeling a little stronger, but knowing I'll be going home soon helps me more than anything else possibly could to feel much better again. I'm so excited I don't pay much attention to all the details Dr. Slusser is telling Miri about how to care for me at home. I'm just *so* happy to be going home again!

My home is a wonderful place, with a magical yard and two dear humans. Being away from home for so long has made me realize just how very special my home is! I feel safe and loved at home. I feel inspired and at peace in my yard. It is my domain, where I'm the one in charge.

I'll tell you more about my yard later.

Home at last

Miri makes me stay in the house for a few days when I first go home because I'm still rather thin and weak. I think that being outside in my yard would help me recover more quickly, but Miri is concerned I might not be strong enough to take care of myself. I don't understand why she is worried about that as I've always felt safe and able to protect myself in my yard. She is right, though, that I'm not yet as strong as usual.

Having to stay indoors makes me think more about Jase because he mostly stayed in the house. Memories of my beloved friend wash through me as I lie here wishing he were lying next to me once more. I miss him so much.

I Get Very Sick

I wish I felt better and I wish I didn't have to get shots of insulin. I wonder whether I will ever feel well and strong again?

Diana still recovering

Chapter 3

SHOTS AND ENERGY SWINGS

Burning sensations spread through my shoulder as Miri gives me another shot of insulin. My muscles tighten so much they hurt more than just where the shot goes through my skin. I'm upset and angry about the pain and because I have no choice about getting shots.

It doesn't feel fair that I have to get a shot every morning and every evening. It doesn't feel fair that Miri won't give me any food until I let her give me a shot. She tells me my body needs the insulin to be able to digest my food. She says I'll get sicker again if I don't have it. I don't want to get sicker again, but I'm not sure it's worth going on living if I have to get two shots every single day for the rest of my life.

I'm used to being healthy, strong, and independent. I've always felt pretty much in control of my life and able to do what I want when I want. Since I lost my mother, the only other time I've felt so powerless like I do now, was when Jase died. I was very unhappy for a long time after losing Jase, and I continue to feel some sadness whenever I think of him.

Jase had always been such a big part of my life that for a while I wasn't sure my life could have meaning without him. But slowly I was able to again enjoy being out in my yard and catching critters. It helped to feel supported by Miri and Wayne's love and caring. And, in those days, I was able to count on my body doing what I wanted it to. I just took it for granted that it would.

Since I got sick with diabetes, I can't count on my body anymore. Much of the time I feel too sick, weak, and tired to do anything other than lay around and sleep. I never know how I'll feel at any moment on any day. I might be feeling pretty good, for a change, and start to think about hunting a mouse again. Then, all of a sudden, I'll feel really bad again. There's no warning. There's nothing I know to do to help myself with this.

The shots of insulin are supposed to help me digest my food so that I'll have energy and feel better. But for the first couple of hours after I get a shot and eat, I usually feel more tired than I did before. Miri explains to me that this is because my blood sugar rises quickly after I eat and the insulin works slowly to bring it back down. She also reminds me that I'm still recovering from being very sick, and that I'm not back to my full strength, yet.

Knowing these things doesn't really help me feel better. Sometimes I just want to cry and cry and cry, but the tears stay stuck in my throat and chest.

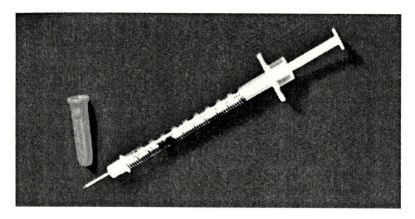

An insulin needle

Shots and Energy Swings

Whenever I know it's about time for me to have a shot, my stomach tightens and feels like it has a huge knot in it. My shoulders become tense and hurt in anticipation of where the shot will to go in, and they continue to feel tight and painful for a while after Miri's given me the shot.

I hate getting shots so much I sometimes hide where Miri can't find me. But then I don't get my food, either. I like to eat and I'm still too weak to catch live prey for myself. So I finally have to give in to her if I'm hungry and want to eat. It's not fair at all.

Miri and Wayne do their best to help me through this hard time by giving me lots of petting, special treats, and explaining to me over and over why I need the shots. Mostly I'm too upset to listen to them. They finally take me to see Samantha, a lady who is able to hear me as well as talk to me. They hope Samantha will be able to help me accept getting shots without becoming so upset.

Samantha first asks me what's happening for me in relation to the shots, and she listens carefully to all that I have to say. I tell her how sick and discouraged I feel and how intensely I hate shots. Samantha also says I do need to have the shots to feel better. She then suggests, when I'm about to get a shot before I eat, that I stand very still and imagine the food on the dish in front of me is a critter I'm about to pounce on.

Focusing in this way, Samantha tells me, will take my attention outside of my body, which will help me not notice the shot so much. As I'm always given food and shots at the same time, this could help me every time I get a shot.

Samantha also tells Miri to change the location on my body each time she gives me a shot. Instead of always placing the shots around my shoulders, she should move them up and down along my back, shoulders and neck. That way no one spot on my body will get so sore and tender, like has been happening.

I have to go back to Dr. Blake and Dr. Slusser many times before I'm feeling well again. I don't mind going to Dr. Blake's, even though he jabs me with acupuncture needles. He's kind, is gentle in his work with me, and talks to me about what he's doing. It feels like he cares about me and tries to understand me.

Dr. Slusser is kind, too, but he doesn't think I can understand him and doesn't explain anything to me. And I don't like staying all day at his office to have my blood drawn every couple of hours. Several different people handle me and take my blood each time, too. That makes it harder to get comfortable with any one person in his office.

Miri says I must have the all day blood testing to find out how much my blood sugar changes throughout a day. Dr. Slusser needs to know this to decide how much insulin to give me so I'll feel as well as possible. Since Miri stays with me all day when I'm at Dr. Slusser's, I know it must be important to stay there that long, as she has lots of other things to do. I'm glad she doesn't leave me there alone. But she doesn't have a needle jabbed into her leg again and again throughout the day to take her blood.

Sometimes I get so mad when Miri hurts me day after day making me have shots that it's hard to believe she really loves me. For a while I feel uneasy and afraid whenever she touches me, and that makes it harder for me to accept and feel supported by her efforts to comfort me. When I finally realize how difficult it is for Miri to give me the shots, I'm able to accept having to get them more easily.

Miri often feels so bad for me that she'll do just about anything I want. I enjoy getting her to give me extra treats and petting by acting more upset than I really feel. That helps a little!

Seeing Wayne take his shots twice a day, just like I have to, helps me accept that I must get shots. Wayne has diabetes, just like me. He patiently explains to me, over and over, that my body needs the insulin in the shot to be able to digest the food I eat. He reminds me that I'll get sicker again if I don't have insulin and assures me I'll gradually continue feeling better if I always have a shot of insulin every morning and evening when I eat.

Wayne also points out to me that the shots don't need to be as big a deal as I'm making them be. I can see that having to take shots isn't that big a deal for him. He also seems to feel pretty well most of the time as long as he remembers to eat and take his shots regularly

Seeing how well he feels and handles having diabetes helps me hang in, hoping this will be true for me, too.

Wayne and Diana resting together.

I wonder if I'll ever feel well and strong again and able to enjoy living like I used to. I wonder whether I'll ever be able to hunt again. Hunting was such an important part of my life. I'm very tired of just watching life go by, being given shots, eating and sleeping.

I do gradually feel better, as Wayne told me would happen. I gain back the weight I lost when I was so very sick. I again take pleasure in sleeping next to Miri and Wayne at night and in simply being near them when they're home during the day. I also once more enjoy being out in my yard feeling the warmth of the sun, watching bees and butterflies buzzing and flitting over flowers, and listening to the songs of birds and crickets. It is so good to just be lying on the earth.

Spending more time in my yard helps me feel more peaceful and better able to handle getting the shots without becoming so upset. I can see that I do feel worse if I miss a shot. Miri works out a better balance of insulin so my blood sugar and energy don't go up and down so much, and that also helps.

There are still times I don't feel very well, but I know now that I will feel better again. I just have to wait for the bad times to pass as my blood sugar comes back to normal. I realize I must eat if I start to feel weak, and a dish of dry food is always out for me.

If I start feeling sorry for myself, I remind myself to do something I know will help me feel better, like going out in my yard and watching critters. Wayne's support and encouragement help me not feel so alone, and his example helps me learn to not pay so much attention to the shots. Even though I didn't believe it could ever be possible, the shots finally become just a "little sting" instead of such a big and painful ordeal.

Most of the time I don't think very much about shots, anymore. They still usually hurt a little and sometimes I cry out. Then Miri hugs and kisses me and tells me how brave I am, and all is okay again in my world.

As more time goes by, I continue to feel stronger as I take it easy and focus on doing those things I can still enjoy. When I'm not outside in my yard, I'm often in the upstairs bedroom resting on the waterbed. I like to lie there next to Miri and Wayne at night and watching the birds eating and fighting at the birdfeeder on the balcony during the day.

As I lie there looking at the birds, I sometimes dream about catching a bird again. In my mind I leap into the air after a dove as it flies away, catching it by the neck, and gliding back down to the earth with it held firmly in my mouth. What joy that would be!

At dusk, two young rats occasionally come and eat at the birdfeeder. In the dim light they can't see me lying on the bed inside and think they won't be noticed. I think about catching one of them, too, and remember what it was like to do so. A rat would taste very good, and having fresh meat to eat would help me feel so much better.

Much as I enjoy observing critters and imagining catching them, it's just not the same as in fact hunting and eating them. It's increasingly hard for me to just be watching. I want to be really hunting again.

Shots and Energy Swings

I wonder whether I'll ever be able to?

Diana in her yard

Chapter 4

HUNTING, MY YARD, AND OTHER JOYS

One evening I'm suddenly awakened from a nap on the waterbed as Miri grabs me and rushes out the balcony door. Saying "Diana, rat," she quickly puts me down. In dazed disbelief, I see a young rat bolt right before my nose headed for a tree branch that hangs low over the tile roof.

By the time the second rat dashes by, I'm after him in a flash, seizing him by the neck just as he leaps from the balcony to the roof. He's dead almost instantly, as I know just how and where to grab his neck to break it.

Joy rushes through me, like an electrical current. I've caught a rat! I've really caught a rat! I wasn't sure I would ever again be able to, but I've just done so, in fact! I can hunt once more, and I'm just as good as I used to be (or, at least, will be very soon)! I feel more fully alive and in my body than I have in a long time. I feel a sense of power and control again.

I carry the rat into the bedroom to show Miri and Wayne. They not only praise me but also allow me to eat him inside. They have never done that before; they've always made me take my prey outside to eat. Now they even place the rat on a towel for me to eat off of, which reminds me of the cloth on the table under their food!

Sinking my teeth deeply into the rat's flesh, I crunch right through bone. I can smell and taste his fresh, pungent blood. Very slowly I devour the rat from head to tail, savoring every mouthful. I leave nothing uneaten, not even the tail. My stomach feels full and warm, and enlivening energy flows through my body.

Hunting has been a central activity for me, ever since I first taught myself how to catch many kinds of "critters," such as mice, rats, lizards, insects, and birds. I've been better at hunting than at anything else I do. Catching mice and rats in the woodpiles, vines, and sheds has been a primary job I've had in my family, as well as one of my greatest pleasures. And having good fresh meat to eat has always helped me feel strong and healthy.

Jase didn't know how to hunt, so I taught myself by finding out what worked. I learned to move silently and quickly and to be very still and quiet in both my body and mind, so that whomever I was stalking wouldn't know I was there. I mastered the ability to extend my awareness beyond my body so I could pick up almost imperceptible sounds, movements, and smells, and thus know exactly what's happening and where.

I know how fast I can run and how far I can leap, as well as how to be so still and silent that no one is aware of my presence. When I finally do go after a critter, it has almost no chance of getting away from me. It often doesn't even know what's happening before I've grabbed and killed it.

At times I've brought some of my prey in for Jase and Miri. Jase occasionally ate part of a mouse or bird. Miri never ate anything I brought her, not even a tender young bird. I don't think she ever even tasted it. I've never fully understood why she wouldn't eat such fine, fresh meat.

Miri says she doesn't want me to catch birds because she enjoys watching birds and hearing them sing. I also like to watch and listen to birds. But they also taste very good, and it feels right for me to hunt and eat birds as well as other critters when I can. So Miri won't feel bad, I mostly hunt birds when she's not at home.

Rats are the most difficult to catch of the critters I hunt because they're usually big and can bite very hard. Their teeth are often as large as mine, and sometimes even larger. I've had to learn exactly where and how to grab them by their necks so they can't bite me. As my jaws are quite strong, I frequently break their necks when I catch them, and then they die quickly.

Sometimes I bring critters into the house, even though Miri and Wayne don't want me to. If a large rat doesn't die immediately when I grab it, I can more easily make sure it won't escape from me before I kill it if I first carry it into the house.

A couple of times a rat got away from me inside the house and ran behind some furniture where I couldn't get to it. Then I've needed Wayne and Miri to help me catch it again, and they weren't too happy about that. Jase always enjoyed tagging along behind us watching the excitement. When Wayne and Miri have had to catch a rat that escaped from me, they always took it away in a bucket and set it free instead of giving it back to me.

I kill with respect for the creature whose life I've taken, and I eat what I catch and kill. I especially enjoy the delicate taste of fresh mice and birds. I also like eating many foods that Miri and Wayne eat, such as chicken, turkey, beef, salmon and other fresh fish, buttered toast, Whoppers, cream, and ice cream. I'm most fond of Arbys.

Now that I've been feeling better and have found out I can catch critters again, I spend more time outside in my yard. It's so good to just be there, lying on the earth, feeling the energy of all the growing plants. When I was sick, I'd almost forgotten how special my yard is.

I remember how excited and overjoyed I was when Miri, Jase and I moved here to live with Wayne and I first saw the big yard behind the house. We'd just had a tiny yard where we lived before. Now there was suddenly so much space all there for me! Back then I was the strongest and fastest cat around, and I made it very clear to any cat who came nearby that this yard was MINE.

My yard is quite beautiful as well as big. In the front part just behind the house are two huge trees with thick rough trunks and widely spreading branches. Many different birds enjoy being in these trees, especially with a birdfeeder nearby on the balcony. In the springtime, the two huge trees are covered with yellow flowers that glow in the sun and cover the ground with a sticky sweet golden blanket when they fall later in the year.

At the back end of Diana's yard

Near the back end of my yard are two smaller trees that have low branches, as well as rambling bushes and many different kinds of weeds. Low vines with purple flowers surround a murky pond that has tall reeds growing in it.

Mosquitoes and other bugs often hang out at the pond, and an occasional red dragonfly comes by, too. I'm most fascinated by dragonflies, and wish they'd visit my pond more often.

Hunting, My Yard and Other Joys

A garage and a little tool shed are near the back of my yard. The garage is filled with boxes of old papers, broken furniture, spiders, mice, and cobwebs. The tool shed has a leaky roof and is damp inside. Many of the tools are all rusty, and some of the wood in the door and walls is rotted.

I can easily go from the roof of our tool shed onto the roof of our neighbor's garage and look over their back yard from above.

I used to enjoy teasing the neighbors' dog from this high vantage point. Since their dog is gone, I still like to check out their yard from above, but I don't go into it as I respect that their yard is the territory of their cats, just as they respect mine.

Next to the little tool shed are a couple of junky woodpiles where mice and rats make their nests. Mice and rats also live in the big shed, and mice and lizards live in the vines surrounding the pond as well as in the dense overgrown bushes covered with pretty blue flowers that are spread all along the fence on the left side of my back yard.

This gives me many places to hunt in, though mostly the big shed is closed and I can only wish I could get in to catch the critters I hear rustling about inside. But I'm kept pretty busy hunting the critters I can get to.

Behind the shed in the back right corner of my yard is a garden where grapes, tomatoes, and figs grow. Branches of lemons hang over the fence from a neighbor's tree. When the figs, grapes, or tomatoes are ripe, many kinds of birds, insects, and lizards come to eat the fruit in the garden, and hunting is good for me.

There's also a small special memorial garden at the back end of the house to the right of the steps that go down from the porch to the yard. In it, a beautiful yellow rosebush grows over the place where Jase's body is buried. Beside the yellow rosebush is a smooth area surrounded by catnip plants for me to lie in the middle of. Beautiful red and purple flowers also grow in Jason's memorial garden. I like to lie with my nose buried in the catnip, watching the bees and butterflies on the flowers.

Lying in Jase's memorial garden

If I want to be alone and hidden, I can curl up in a nest of branches and leaves beneath some dense bushes behind the pond. Another of my favorite places is lying on the porch in a low cardboard box that is a perfect fit for me. As I can see most of my yard when I lie curled in this box, it's a good place from which to watch over my domain. Or I can go and make my rounds to check whether anyone else has left their scent in my yard and to make sure all is okay.

Hunting, My Yard and Other Joys

A large bright blue bird with a loud raucous voice often comes to visit my yard. He likes to tease me, and it's fun for me to watch and listen to him. This is one bird I don't really try hard to catch because I enjoy him so much.

Sometimes skunks and opossums hang out in my yard, too. Skunks can make an awful stink and possums can give a nasty bite, so I just let them be and they do the same for me. Once in a while opossums come into our house to eat my dry food, which is always out because I need to eat something whenever I start to feel weak.

A couple of times a baby opossum has taken up residence behind the dryer, which is around the corner from my food and water in the kitchen. They explore the house at night and have an easy life, until Miri or Wayne notices the stinky mess behind the dryer, sees them wandering about the house in the dark, or is surprised by one of them stuck in a toilet.

I enjoy just being with Miri and Wayne, whatever they are doing. They let me know they are glad I'm with them, too. I curl up next to them on the couch if they are reading, or on the table or desk if they are working on paperwork there. Sometimes Miri comes out in my yard to water or trim flowers and bushes, and of course I'm right with her. Wayne plays the piano most beautifully, and it's a joy to be able to lie and listen to his playing.

I also have a game I like to play with Wayne. When it's time for Miri and Wayne to eat, I try to get to his chair at the table before he does. If he beats me there, I wait nearby. Then, if he gets up to fetch something, I sneak onto his chair and settle down.

Wayne always exclaims, "Diana!" when he sees me, moves the chair I'm on over towards Miri, and gets himself another one.

Sometimes Miri and Wayne just put a chair between them for me ahead of time, which is nice, but playing the game with Wayne is much more fun.

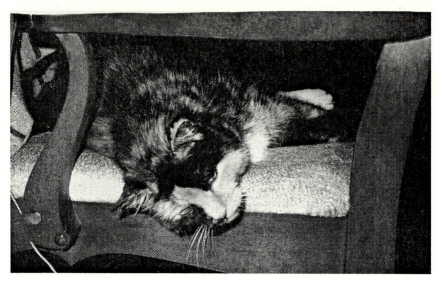

On Wayne's chair

I enjoy being indoors when Miri and Wayne are at home, but when I'm alone I'm mostly out in my yard. I often just lie on the moist earth under the big trees and feel the cool breeze or the warmth of the sun.

As I lie in my yard I can smell the sage, rosemary, and other plants, listen to the songs of the birds, the buzzing of the bees, the wind-chimes on the balcony upstairs, and the rustling of the breeze among the leaves, and watch the sunlight as it shimmers its way magically through the branches making ever-changing patterns of light and shadow on the ground below. Every plant and every animal has its own special energy.

In my yard I always feel happy and at peace. If I'm in the house and start to feel sad, lonely, or unwell, I just go outside and find something to do, watch, or listen to. Being outdoors always helps me feel better and more alive again.

I especially love being out in my yard in the golden red glowing light of dusk when all the critters are out and about, and the crickets are chirping their soothing chorus. The evening is a very special time for me.

Hunting, My Yard and Other Joys

All is well for me again in my yard...until I have an unexpected visitor.

Diana's hunting grounds

Chapter 5

A STRANGER HUNTS IN MY YARD

One evening when I go out into my yard at dusk, someone I've never seen before is hunting by the woodpile behind the tool shed. He's grayish brown with darker markings on his face and tail, about my size, and unlike any animal I've ever seen. His long thin face is similar in shape to an opossum's, but his ears are long and pointed and his tail is much more bushy than an opossum's. He's crouching over a mouse he just killed.

I want to let this stranger know he's in my territory. Very slowly, but firmly and confidently I approach him, as I would another cat. He glares at me angrily, and then suddenly, with no warning, lunges at me with such speed and force that I'm thrown off balance. For a moment I'm too shocked to move, as I've never experienced anything like this before. As I turn to run away, he grabs my back leg in his needle sharp teeth and intense pain tears through my leg. I bite and claw him as hard as I can. He lets go of my leg and backs away when he realizes how well I can fight.

Terrified, I dash for the house. This stranger is very strong and is filled with rage. I think he would like to kill and eat me, but fortunately I'm too good a fighter. I get safely into the house, but am trembling all over and can't stop yucky smelling inky black poop from running out of me all over the kitchen floor and rug. Miri will be very upset when she sees and smells it.

I'm afraid the angry stranger will somehow be able to find me and hurt me more. I crawl away into a very small space behind some boxes in a closet where there's no way he could possibly get to me. My leg is bleeding and throbbing intensely with pain, and my body is still shaking uncontrollably. I don't know what to do to help or take care of myself.

I didn't expect this being to lunge at me with such force and knock me off my feet. I wasn't being fierce or mean to him, just letting him know that this is my yard. I've never been attacked like this or so badly injured before in my life.

This stranger has taken away my feeling of being capable and on top of things. I feel sick in my heart and terrible about myself, like I've badly failed at protecting my yard and taking care of myself. I'm ashamed of the mess I made on the kitchen floor and about having gotten hurt so badly.

Before this happened, I felt able to protect myself and guard my yard. The only time I didn't was when I first got diabetes and was too sick to do anything. I've always been able to handle whatever happens in my yard, and I've earned the respect of any other cats who come around. Except for opossums and skunks, who come and go as they wish, no one else has been able to hunt in my yard unless I let them, as I've done with one cat who was very thin and hungry.

I'm scared Miri and Wayne won't want to have me around anymore. They are calling and looking for me now, and sound very concerned. I yearn for their comfort and help, but I'm afraid they'll be very angry with me for making such a mess on the floor. Except for the time I first caught a rat again on the balcony after being so sick, they haven't allowed me to eat critters in the house because their blood stains the carpets. This is a far worse mess than that made by any critter's blood.

Miri must know how badly I feel about the mess I made on the kitchen floor. She's saying she doesn't care about the mess, but just wants to be with me and know I'm okay. I want to believe her.

After a long time, I finally risk coming out of hiding and limp over to where Miri fell asleep on the couch. She senses my presence and awakens, picks me up, and holds me for a long long time, stroking and comforting me. My body continues shaking, and Miri knows something terrible has happened to me. She's clearly very glad to see me, and that is reassuring. I feel safe in her arms, and gradually my body begins to relax and stops trembling.
Miri realizes my leg is hurt when she sees me limp as I walk. She carefully examines my leg, thoroughly cleans it, and puts some ointment on it that burns like fire. She explains that the ointment will kill the germs and help it get better, so I hold as still as I can in spite of the pain.

Miri is very angry at whoever hurt me. She tells me she'll catch the culprit and take him so far away he'll never be able to find his way back. That's nice to hear, but he's so quick I can't imagine any way she can possibly do that. She isn't as fast as she used to be, and she was never nearly as fast as the angry stranger.

By the next morning my leg is fat, puffy, and much too painful to walk on. Miri takes me to see Dr. Blake, who says my leg has become infected. He cleans away the yellow puss oozing from the holes in my leg where I was bitten. It hurts badly when he squeezes my leg to force the puss out, but I know he's trying to help me and hold as still as I can. Like Miri did, Dr. Blake puts burning salve on my leg, and sends pills and more ointment along home with Miri to give to me.

My leg stays swollen and painful for a long time, in spite of having the pills and ointment several times every day. It hurts too much to do anything but lie around, and I get so discouraged I just want to crawl away somewhere and hide. If it weren't for Miri and Wayne's love and caring, I don't know what I would do.

I wish Jase were still here with me. I could sure use the comfort of his warm body and loving spirit right now. Sometimes I imagine I'm curled up next to him again, and that helps me feel a little better.

During the time I'm feeling so disheartened, we again meet with Samantha. While Samantha and I are discussing what might help me fill my time in a meaningful way, the idea of my sharing with children about all I've been through comes up. I'd like to do this if it could possibly help a child who is going through similar experiences to hear my story.

One day I overhear Miri and Wayne discussing my leg. They think it hasn't healed yet because I have diabetes, and they sound very concerned that I could possibly lose my leg if something more isn't done soon to help it heal. Hearing them say that is very upsetting to me. I can't imagine being without one of my legs.

Miri asks Dr. Blake for stronger medicine, and he gives her some very powerful antibiotic shots for her to give me for a couple of weeks. The new shots require a larger syringe with a thicker needle than my insulin shots do, and they burn worse, too. I feel like screaming and fighting when Miri gives them to me, but I put up with them because she says they'll help my leg get better. I so much want my leg to be okay again.

My leg does finally start feeling better after I've had the stronger shots for several days. The puffiness gradually goes down, and I'm able to walk without so much pain. It feels so good to be able to move around more freely again!

I feel scared and uneasy whenever I go out in my yard, now. I stay close to the house, and always carefully check out the whole yard to make sure the angry stranger who attacked me isn't there. Sometimes Miri goes out with me, and that helps me feel safer. I think it's good for her to be outside more, too.

A Stranger Hunts in My Yards

Miri thinks a mean cat I've had growling spats with lately is the one who attacked me. This nasty cat has been around more since my leg was injured. He knows I've been hurt, and is trying to take over my yard. He's even dared to come inside the house a couple of times. Whenever Miri sees the mean cat in our house, she tries to beat him to the cat door to trap him inside. She also yells at him and chases him whenever she sees him in my yard.

I don't like the mean cat, but he's not the one who hurt me, and I'm not afraid of him. Even though I've been hurt, I can still fight another cat if I have to.

I haven't seen the angry stranger since the day he seized my leg with his piercing teeth. I'm just starting to feel a little more comfortable being in my yard again when suddenly, one evening just as it's getting dark, there he is. I dash for the house as fast as I can. He lunges after me and again grabs my leg. Yowling loudly, I bite and claw him hard. He lets go as one of my claws digs deeply into his nose and backs off, slinking away behind the garage.

Miri hears my yowl and comes running out of the house, screaming loudly after my attacker. She's furious that I've been hurt again. I am, too. The next day Miri brings home a big trap and sets it up in the back yard. She explains to me what it's for, and I know better than to go inside it even though there's some fresh chicken in it that I'd like to have.

An opossum gets caught in the trap the first night. Miri lets her go free, as opossums have always been around and I get along with them okay. The angry being who hurt me is caught the second night, and I hear him furiously yipping and moving about in the trap. Although the trap is secure and he isn't able to get himself out, I watch from a safe distance right outside the cat door.

In the morning, Miri is quite surprised when she sees what kind of animal is in the trap. She tells me he's a "fox", and that she had no idea a fox could get into our yard. She carries me over near the cage to show me he's been caught, saying he probably wanted to kill and eat me. I'd already realized that from the way he lunged at me and seized my leg with no warning.

I didn't know, before this happened, that there were animals who would want to eat me; I'd always been the one doing the hunting and eating of others.

Mr. fox

Making sure I'm watching her, Miri puts the trap with the fox inside it into the car. She tells me she is taking the fox far away in the country, so far away there's no way he can ever find his way back and hurt me again. She drives away with the fox in the trap and is gone a long time. When she comes back, the trap is empty.

After carefully examining the fence all the way around my yard, Miri finds a hole behind the garage that is large enough for the small fox to fit through. She puts a great big thick board over the hole and fastens it there. She assures me that no fox can ever come through the fence into my yard and hurt me again.

I'm glad Miri took the fox far away and fixed the fence. But, in spite of her doing so, I still have bad dreams about being hurt for a long time after the fox is gone. I'm also easily frightened by any sound I'm not expecting or don't recognize.

A Stranger Hunts in My Yards

I long to feel safe and comfortable in my yard again, like I always did before. I wonder whether I ever will?

Diana Living Through Life's Challenges

Diana by her post.

Chapter 6

MY LIFE GOES ON

Since the angry fox attacked and hurt me, I continue to feel uneasy when I'm out in my yard. Miri seemed SO sure of herself when she told me she took the fox much too far away for him to ever find his way back to my yard. Although I saw her take him away inside the trap, saw her bring the trap back empty, and saw her securely cover the hole in the fence, I'm still constantly watching and listening for any unusual sound or movement if I go out.

I'm not able to just relax and enjoy being in my yard like I used to. I'm not sure I can protect myself anymore. That's very difficult for me, as I've always felt confident and safe in my yard before the fox injured me.

When my leg hurts and I don't feel up to doing anything, I remember with fond longing the warmth and comfort of Jase's body snuggled next to mine. Before the fox's attack, I would just go outside and find something to occupy myself with whenever I missed Jase. But now, especially when my leg hurts, I remember my experience with the fox and am scared to go outside. At such times I miss Jase more than ever.

In spite of my uneasiness, I begin to go outside more again. When the fox has really not come back after many days go by, I gradually start to feel safer being out in my yard again. I'm very glad about that, as my yard has always been a very healing place to spend time in.

My leg slowly continues to get better, but it never becomes fully okay the way it used to be. It still hurts if the weather is rainy or when I run, though the pain doesn't get real bad, anymore. I'm very grateful to be able to again walk around fairly comfortably. I can't move as quickly as I used to or hunt as easily or well, either. But I can still run if I have to, and I can hunt a little, too.

In some ways it's been good to be inside the house more when Miri and Wayne are at home. They've gone out of their way to pet me, talk to me, give me all my favorite foods, and tell me how much they love me and are glad I'm here with them. I enjoy just being near them during the day and lying on the bed next to them at night. I like to feel special to them and it's nice to not have to be concerned about Jase getting jealous whenever they express their caring for me.

Hanging out with Wayne

Since Jase is gone, I've come to more fully realize just how special my relationship with Miri and Wayne is. They have always been important to me, but I now feel even more strongly the goodness of the bond of love we share.

Something very basic has changed for me. Going outside and being in my yard again isn't my only source of pleasure, now.

I'm more aware of how important it is to feel connected to others, and of how much I need to have love and closeness in my life. I kind of took those things for granted, before.

Losing Jase hurt so much I didn't want to get too close to anyone again for a long time after his death. But Miri and Wayne's constant expressions of their love for me throughout the time I was so sick and hurt deeply reassured me of their love for me just as I am, even though I can't hunt well anymore.

I've come to realize I don't need to be a strong super cat always on top of everything to be special and worthwhile. Miri and Wayne love me just for me!

Sometimes it's still hard for me to fully accept this, but when I let it in it's like a warm fuzzy feeling that spreads all through me. I mostly don't try not to need anyone, now, like I did for a long time after losing Jase. I've come to trust Miri and Wayne's love and caring.

For quite some time after Jase died, I often felt like he was still here. Sometimes the sense of his presence was so strong that I would look up, expecting to see him in his body. Then I'd feel sad and disappointed when I couldn't see him with my eyes, as the feeling of his being here with me was so very real.

Samantha helped me realize that Jase can still be with us in his spirit, even though his body is no longer here. Knowing this allowed me to appreciate the goodness of his energetic, spiritual presence here with me, even though I couldn't see his body.

Then, for a long period of time, I didn't experience Jase being around very much. I tried not to think a lot about him, and kept myself busy with hunting and watching over my yard. But I still missed Jase especially while I was recovering from nearly dying, when I was coming to terms with having diabetes, and again after the fox hurt my leg.

Lately I've been feeling Jase's spirit around more, and Miri has been sensing his presence, too. She has the impression that Jase wants to come back and be with us again, and asks me whether I'd want him to return and be with us once more.

Miri hasn't learned to understand me very well, yet, so we meet with Samantha to talk more about Jase's possible return. As did Miri, Samantha asks me how I'd feel about Jase coming back? She explains to me that he would return as a baby in a new body, and that he would look different and have to grow up all over.

I'm not sure I fully understand what this would be like. I can vaguely remember curling up next to my sister when we were babies, just like I always did with Jase. But much more clearly than with my sister, I remember the comfort of Jase's presence, of being snuggled next to his warm furry body, of tenderly licking each other's faces, and of feeling like he would always be there for me.

Because I so deeply miss Jase in all these ways, I tell Samantha I would very much like to have him back with us again.

When Miri felt that Jase wanted to return to us, she told him she would need his help to make this happen, as she didn't know any female cats who could have babies. A day or two later, Miri got a phone call from Stephanie, the woman she gets my food from. Stephanie asked Miri if she knew of anyone who would give a good home to a kitten. She was caring for an injured pregnant wild mother cat, and would need to find homes for the babies.

Miri got all excited and shivery when Stephanie told her this. I do, too, when Miri tells me what Stephanie shared with her. Miri asks Samantha whether Jase could come back to us through this mother cat, and Samantha tells her Jase's spirit is already connected to the body of one of the unborn kittens.

Before the kittens are born, Miri and Wayne take me to meet the mother cat, and we then all meet again with Samantha. I don't like the mother cat, and I don't want her in my home.

Samantha assures me that the mother cat will not need to be in my home. She explains to me that a very tiny Jase is growing inside the mother cat's belly and in several months he will come out of her as a baby. The mother cat will have to care for him until he's big and strong enough to eat food on his own, and then he can come and live with us again.

Samantha also tells me that Jase's body and his personality will be different in some ways. As a kitten, he will be smaller than when I knew him and full of playful energy, not tired and weak like he was at the end of his last life. She assures me that he will have a very loving spirit like he had when he was here with me before, whatever all else may be different about him.

I so very much want to have Jase's love and his comforting physical presence back with me again that I don't pay a lot of attention to most of the things Samantha says about all of the ways Jase will be different than he was before. I just remember all of the things I miss about how he was when we were together.

I get both excited and anxious whenever I think about Jase being back with us again. I'm a little afraid of losing some of the special status I've come to feel with Miri and Wayne. I didn't like Jase's jealousy when Miri and Wayne gave me attention.

But the fact is that Miri and Wayne are both gone much of the time. I'm not young anymore, and I often don't feel very well. The thought of again having the support and comfort of Jase's love and presence is most welcome. For these reasons I'd like to have him back, even if he has to return as a small kitten in a new body.

After the baby kittens are born, Miri and Wayne spend time playing with them every week. They tell me that they always feel more connected to one particular kitten more than any of the others, even though five of the seven kittens look so much alike that it's hard to tell them apart. They also feel some connection to a second kitten, but not as strongly as to the first one.

Miri and Wayne take pictures of these two kittens that they feel most strongly connected with to show Samantha, without telling her anything about them. On one of the photos they mark "X" and on the other "O". Miri says Samantha immediately pointed to the picture with the "X", saying the spirit of Jason is in that one. Kitten "X" is the same one Miri and Wayne both feel more strongly connected to.

The baby kittens

Jase is in a female body this time, Miri tells me. Wayne thinks of "Jada" as a new name for him/her. He came up with this name by putting "JA" from the beginning of Jason together with "DA" from the word Daughter (because Jase is a girl, now). I like that the new name has the "JA" sound in it, like Jase's name had.

Miri builds a little house out of boxes for baby Jada. She built one for me, too, when I was a baby, but I think Jada's house is nicer than mine was. Mine didn't have a pointed roof covered with thick rug material that's so easy and fun to climb up on, but was just made out of plain old cardboard boxes. Miri puts Jada's house in front of the fireplace in the living room.

Then one day Miri tells me she and Wayne are going to Stephanie's and that they will be bringing baby Jada back with them when they return. I await their return with restless, eager anticipation. When I hear the car pull up outside I feel a little anxious, but mostly rather excited.

My Life Goes On

Will they really have Jase with them again as Jada? Will s/he remember me?

Baby Jada

Chapter 7

JADA ARRIVES

I hear Miri and Wayne bringing baby Jada in the front door. Quietly but quickly I sneak under the kitchen table so I can take a look at her without being seen. I don't believe my eyes. A fluffy, bouncy, tiny gray kitten who is supposed to be Jason come back to be with us again is running about, checking everything out.

I feel dismayed and disappointed. There must be a mistake, or I've been tricked or betrayed. This kitten can't possibly be Jase. Miri and Wayne are playing with her now and don't even notice me watching. They don't look around for me and obviously aren't thinking about me at all. I feel left out and unimportant.

Even though Jase was jealous and possessive of Wayne and Miri's attention, I always knew he loved me a lot. And I know Miri and Wayne love me too, especially with all the attention and care they gave me while I was so sick. But now I'm afraid this baby Jada will become the special one to Miri and Wayne. I'm afraid I won't matter as much to them, anymore. This is not working out the way it was supposed to, at all.

At some point Miri finally notices me under the table and calls out: *"Diana, come and meet Jada."* Then baby Jada sees me, too. She runs towards me excitedly as though she expects I'll be delighted to see her.

I quickly get up and hiss at Jada, warning her to keep her distance. I continue hissing at her over my shoulder as I make a hasty retreat. Jada stops in her tracks when I hiss, and draws back, surprised. She must have truly believed I'd be glad to see her. I was looking forward to seeing her, in fact, but I thought she'd be more like Jase was.

Jase was calm and gentle. Though he got jealous easily, he also needed and respected me. Above all, I knew he deeply loved me. Jase would never have rushed towards me so quickly as Jada does, unless we were playing. The only other being who ever dashed at me in that way was the fox, and the fox's attack was by far the most terrifying experience I've ever had in my life.

Even though I know this tiny baby can't hurt me like the fox did, it's upsetting to be rushed at like that, by someone I don't know.

Baby Jada is small, quick, and bouncy. Jase was big and moved about very slowly and cautiously, at least in his later years. Jase's eyes were an attractive bright shade of blue, and hers are a dull yellowish green. His fur was a beautiful light tan color, while she is mostly gray and white. Jada does have some dark markings on her face that are sort of like Jase's markings were, and she does have a fluffy striped tail like he had. Those are the only similarities I can see. Overall, she doesn't really look or seem like him at all.

Because of her size, baby Jada reminds me more of my sister than she does of Jase. My sister was the only other kitten this small I've ever known. But my sister was also a beautiful golden tan color, more like Jase. Remembering the pain of having been separated from my sister makes it hard for me to imagine letting myself get close to such a tiny being again.

Miri asks me to remember how Jase was with me when I was a baby. She would like me to care for and play with this baby Jada in the ways Jase did with me, but I can not imagine doing so. Right now I need comfort and love like I used to get from Jase, not to have to take care of a baby.

Jada Arrives

Even though Samantha told me Jase would come back in a new baby's body, I still expected he would be much more like he was as Jase than this kitten is.

When I was little, Jase allowed me to pounce on him, bite him, and hold him down, pretending I was bigger and stronger than he. Jase licked my face and body all over, like my mother used to do, and he let me snuggle up close to him when we rested.

I enjoyed running up to Jase, batting him, and then dashing quickly away before he could bat me back. I'd keep on doing this until he chased me or batted me. When he'd had enough playing and wanted to rest, he'd give me that very stern look of his. If I kept on teasing him after he gave me his look, he would give me a very hard swat with his paw.

It's wonderful to remember how Jase played with and cared for me, but I can't imagine being like that with this baby Jada. I'm not young and full of energy like I used to be. I'm not old, but I'm getting to be more elderly and am often tired and wanting to just lie quietly and not be bothered. And when my leg is hurting or I'm not feeling well, it makes me feel even worse about myself to see Jada darting about, obviously feeling good and full of energy.

I agreed to Jase coming back because I wanted to have the comfort, closeness, and love we used to have back again. This Jada's constant activity is hard for me to handle, or even to be around very much. It certainly doesn't feel comforting or loving, like I was expecting and longing for.

I really don't like how Jada seems to be trying to take over everything. She thinks she owns the place and can have whatever she wants. Jase also had some of that attitude, but Jada is much worse than he was. Miri keeps telling me I am the first cat, now. She says I should just stand up to Jada and let her know when I'm not okay with something she's doing. But it's really hard for me to do that all the time, and I mean ALL THE TIME.

Although I missed Jase, I also enjoyed being Miri and Wayne's only cat. It was good to feel more special to them. I'm sorry now that I agreed to Jada coming to be with us, whether or not she is really Jase. I wish she would just go away.

Diana Living Through Life's Challenges

My heart cries out to Miri: *"Please take Jada away! I want to be the only special one to you and Wayne."*

But baby Jada does not go away. For some time, I'm able to avoid being around her very much. She mostly stays out in the living room, so I go to the back part of the house, upstairs, or outside in my yard. But then Miri starts taking me into the living room next to Jada. She stays with us, trying to make us get used to being near each other. Miri talks on and on about how good it could be for us both if we became close like Jase and I used to be.

Gradually I begin to feel a little more comfortable around Jada, and we start lying near each other on the couch. Jada enjoys reaching out to touch the end of my tail. I flick my tail around when I'm not totally relaxed, which I'm certainly not when she's lying near me. I don't like to have her touching my tail, and hiss at her when she does.

Jada reaching for Diana's tail

At first Jada backs off when I hiss, as she did when we first met. Then she realizes she can make me hiss by touching my tail, and keeps on doing so over and over. This makes me really mad, so I growl at her. She at first backs off when I growl, but soon even growling doesn't stop her from trying to get a rise out of me.

Jada Arrives

Miri stops Jada from teasing me when she is with us. But as soon as Jada and I are again alone together, she resumes her game of trying to make me mad. I don't find it funny, at all.

One day Jada runs straight at me and pounces on top of me. That does it, as far as I'm concerned. I've totally had it with trying to get along with her. Insulted, frustrated, and angry, I don't want anything more to do with her.
Ever.
I refuse to let Miri carry me out into the living room to be with Jada, anymore. I'm so angry I think I might hurt Jada if Miri made me be with her, and I think Miri knows this. Miri and Wayne don't know what to do. Because I'm so upset, they close the door between the living room and the rest of the house to keep Jada from coming to wherever I am. Miri stops taking me into the living room near her.
For awhile.
Then one day the door that usually keeps us separate is left wide open. I don't see Jada, so I wander cautiously out into the living room to check things out. Jada isn't there. I hope she is gone for good, but Miri brings her back home again in the evening.

Miri explains to me that Jada isn't feeling well because she had an operation so she won't have babies. She says Jada needs to rest and recover from her operation and will be too weak and tired to jump on me for a few days. Miri thinks this is a good time for Jada and me to get used to being around each other, and very firmly tells both Jada and me that we have to learn to live together and will be spending time with each other every day from now on.
With some misgivings, I allow Miri to again carry me into the living room and put me on the couch near Jada, like she used to do. Jada doesn't look like she's feeling very well. She is quieter than usual, and sleeps most of the time. She seems more like Jase was during the last years of his life. I don't mind being around Jada when she's quiet like this.
While Jada is recovering, we lie calmly near each other on the couch for hours at a time. But as soon as she begins to feel stronger, she starts teasing me again.

Jada about to pounce

If either Miri or Wayne sees Jada trying to jump on me, they put her into the "calliboose" (cat carrier) or in a room by herself with the door closed. Jada doesn't like to be penned up or alone, so she learns to not pounce on me if they're nearby. But when Miri and Wayne aren't around to put her in the calliboose, she continues teasing and pestering me. I have to hide or go outside if I don't want to be jumped on when she and I are alone.

Miri encourages me to swat Jada hard when she pesters me too much. She reminds me that I am the first cat now, the queen, and that I have the right to be wherever I want to be. Miri also points out to me how much bigger I am than Jada and suggests I take charge while Jada is still smaller than I am, so she'll learn that I am boss. I do swat Jada a couple of times, but she soon learns to stay out of my reach.

It's really hard for me to stand up to Jada over and over when she keeps on bugging me for what seems like forever. I also don't want to be too hard on Jada, as I now recognize Jase in her sometimes. If he is really back with us in this Jada, I want him to know I still love him.

Jada Arrives

Jada teasing Diana

Most of the time it's easier for me to stay out of Jada's way as much as I can rather than have to repeatedly stand my ground with her. But that allows her to be top cat in whatever parts of the house she most wants to be. Then I can't hang out there unless I'm willing to put up with being teased, often until I'm too upset to take it anymore.

Jada doesn't bug me when I'm out in my yard, so I spend a lot of my time there. I think she feels uneasy being in the yard because she was sprayed by a skunk the very first day she went outside.

I got a good laugh out of that! Jada was so sure of herself, but the skunk put her in her place. I wish I could find a way to do that so quickly and easily as the skunk did.

Miri sets up an appointment with a lady named Sue to talk with Jada and me because Samantha isn't well and can't meet with us. Sue can hear and understand animals, like Samantha does. Miri hopes Sue will be able to help us get along better.

Diana Living Through Life's Challenges

Sue tells Miri to get a feather-bird toy that whirls around on a string at the end of a fishing pole for Jada to chase. She says this kind of toy will give Jada another way to work off her hotrod-like energy other than by pouncing on me. I like that idea very much! Miri gets a whirling bird toy for Jada, and Jada greatly enjoys chasing it.

As long as Miri remembers to play with Jada and her new bird toy every day, she doesn't pounce on me. I also enjoy watching Jada chase the bird toy, so this helps us both feel better.

I start to like Jada more after she stops pouncing on me. It now feels good to have her playing nearby. I still don't trust her fully, and she also keeps her distance from me much of the time, too. But now we often touch noses and smell, kiss, or lick each other. We are more comfortable being around each other, and often lie near each other when we're resting.

Diana and Jada lying near each other

Now that Jada is calmer, I can see that she does have a very loving spirit like Jase had, although she doesn't express her love so openly and actively as he did. Jada has the same way of looking deeply and directly into my eyes that Jase had. It feels like she's looking into my soul, as it did with him.

Jada Arrives

Also like Jase, Jada is jealous of any attention that Miri and Wayne give to me. I'm also jealous of attention they give her more than I was with Jase, probably because I got more from him. But this mostly isn't a problem, as Miri and Wayne make sure to give us both equal attention as much as possible.

I stand up to Jada enough to claim back being in some of my favorite places in the house, though it's too hard to do so with everywhere I like to be. Jada especially doesn't want me to hang out in the upstairs bedroom where Miri and Wayne sleep. It's harder for me to climb the stairs now, so I've mostly just allowed her to have the upstairs as her special place.

Miri is upset that I seldom go upstairs anymore, as she knows how much I enjoy going out on the tile roof and sleeping near her and Wayne at night. I miss sleeping near them, but I'm okay staying mostly downstairs. I still go up if I know the balcony door is open or if I want to lie near them and feel up to dealing with Jada's pestering.

I continue to clearly be queen of the outdoors. Jada is not much better at hunting than Jase was. She can only catch flies, long legged spiders, and occasionally a lizard. She eats the flies and spiders, but just plays with the lizards until they die and then leaves them lying there. Miri takes lizards away from her whenever she sees her playing with them, if they aren't too badly hurt.

I've always eaten what I catch, and as you know, eating freshly caught critters helped me feel stronger and healthier.

Miri and Wayne would like Jada to learn to hunt, and ask me if I will teach her. I'm not sure I want or feel able to even try to teach Jada anything about hunting. I had to teach myself all I know by finding out what worked, and she can do the same.

It's a lot harder for me to hunt now than it used to be since my leg often hurts, I can't run as fast as I used to, and I can't see very well, anymore. And I don't think Jada would really want me to teach her how to hunt, or, for that matter, how to do anything. She often watches me, but thinks she knows best about everything. She doesn't realize how little she knows about hunting, though.

I have to laugh to myself when I see Jada trying to catch a critter. She simply doesn't know how to keep her body and mind still enough to not be seen and heard.

Maybe Jada will be able to learn more about hunting on her own, over time, like I did. I'd be willing to share more with her if she would truly want to listen to me and learn from me. I realize that Jada hasn't seen me hunting very often, and never when I was at my best, so she doesn't really have any idea how good a hunter I used to be or how much I do know.

Jada

Jada Arrives

It is fun for me to watch Jada, now. She's so full of enthusiasm and energy she has to be moving whenever she's not resting. She continues to tease me occasionally, but not in the mean way she used to. Mostly I enjoy watching and being near her, and I'm glad she's here with us.

Diana Living Through Life's Challenges

Diana looking out over her yard

Chapter 8

REFLECTIONS

I used to take everything in my life for granted before I lost my beloved Jase, got sick with diabetes, was attacked by the angry fox, and had Jada become part of my family. Because of these challenges, I've had to take a deeper look at what my life is really about and find new sources of joy and meaning.

I've always done whatever I could to help out my family. I still contribute what I can, but many of the ways I'm able to do so now are different than they were before.

Earlier in my life I used to bring Miri prey I had caught (which she didn't appreciate), and other things that I thought she might like or be able to use such as pretty leaves, interesting pieces of wood, half-packages of cigarettes (she smoked back then), a metal tape measure, and a small plastic shovel.

Miri made a beautiful arrangement of some of the leaves and wood I've brought her, and she still has it in a central place in her special room. I'm glad she likes my presents enough to keep them where she can see them everyday and that she also shows them to others. I continue to bring Miri presents of unusual leaves and pieces of wood.

Diana Living Through Life's Challenges

Jada behind arrangement of Diana's gift leaves

When Miri, Jase, and I went to live with Wayne, it became my job to watch over the back yard and to hunt rats and mice in the woodpiles, bushes, vines, and sheds. I was very good at hunting back then. Hunting gave me excitement, challenge and pleasure in addition to helping out my family.

I'm not as good at hunting or protecting my yard anymore since I can't run or see very well, my leg often aches where it was injured, and I don't always feel well, especially when my blood sugar swings. So I've had to find some other ways of enjoying life and feeling useful and needed.

Being out in my yard and catnip garden still provide ongoing pleasures for me. I also continue to greatly enjoy eating, especially the white mice Miri occasionally brings me. They give me a chance to kill and eat fresh food even though I can't catch prey on my own in the wild anymore. Having freshly killed meat helps me feel better, and the remnant of hunting gives me joy.

I enjoy watching and being with Jada, too, now that she's slowed down some and doesn't pounce on me anymore. I'm sorry it was so hard for me to accept her at first. I realize now how much it hurt Jada that I couldn't accept and welcome her, and how hard it still is for her to trust me because of this.

I can see Jase more clearly in Jada, now, and I truly like her and think she's pretty neat. Sometimes she still bugs me, but then I am also crabby when I don't feel well. I usually am not up to playing with her in the active ways she would like. She's more able to accept this, but I don't think she fully understands the basic differences there are in our energy because of my health problems and how much older I am than she is.

Jada's incredible energy was simply too much for me, at first. Her speed and the way she ran at and jumped on me reminded me of the angry fox who grabbed and hurt my leg so badly, and brought back some memories and pain from that experience. And my initial disappointment that Jada wasn't more obviously like Jase didn't help me accept her.

Looking back, I think there was just too big a difference in what Jada and I expected and needed, because of the contrast in our ages and energies, for us to accept each other as we were.

I can see now that I was not the only one badly hurt by those early experiences Jada and I had with each other. We each got too caught up in our own needs and pain to realize how much the other was also hurting. I don't think either one of us meant to hurt each other like we did. I'm deeply sorry it was so painful for both of us, and hope Jada and I will continue to get closer and be able to forgive and trust each other more.

It's hard to realize how much I've hurt someone whose soul I deeply love without having meant to, because I was so caught up in my own fear and pain. I wish I could make it up to Jada in some way. That's part of why I don't always stand up to her now as much as I otherwise might, even when I do feel up to doing so.

Miri keeps reminding me that I need to take care of my own needs, too. She says I'll resent Jada having whatever I give up to her, if I don't. I know that is sometimes true, and I'm trying to find a balance between the two. I'm also trying to find more ways to let Jada know I truly like and enjoy her now.

I've learned that it's okay for me to feel hurt, angry, or sad, and that I'll feel worse later if I just shut off my feelings. I've also learned how important it is to enjoy life and feel good about myself and about those things I can do well or have done well. Like, even though I can't hunt very well anymore, I know I used to be really good at it. I can still feel some of the pleasures of hunting when Miri brings me a mouse to kill and eat.

At first it was very hard for Miri to bring me a live mouse because she felt bad for it when I killed it. She and Wayne used to take any critter I'd caught away from me if it wasn't too badly hurt when they first saw it.

After I got sick with diabetes, Miri and Wayne not only stopped taking critters away from me, but also carried me out on the balcony to help me catch my first rat after I'd been too weak to hunt for so long. They'd come to realize how essential hunting was to me and knew how much better I would feel if I caught, killed, and ate a rat again. I think they also understood in a new way how hunting and eating other creatures is a part of the cycle of life.

You humans also eat critters, just as I do, whenever you eat meat. Maybe you forget that what you're eating was once a living being because most of you don't hunt and kill your own food?

Diana and a curious mouse

Reflections

Sometimes the white mice Miri brings me don't seem to realize I'm about to kill and eat them and and are curious about me instead of running away. Once one of them even put his nose up to touch mine. That never happened to me before in all my years of hunting, and sometimes I feel a tiny bit bad about killing them.

Since the fox attacked me, I know what it's like to have another being try to kill you and want to eat you. I also know how much better I feel when I have fresh food to eat. It has always felt right for me to hunt and it still does, so I go ahead and kill and eat the mice Miri brings me.

And I enjoy them very much.

I can always help myself feel better by focusing my attention on those things I enjoy and feel good about rather than on having diabetes, getting shots, the pain in my leg, or not being able to hunt well anymore.

I've had to accept that I have diabetes, that I sometimes don't feel very well, and that I must get shots twice a day when I eat or I'll feel worse. At first it was hard for me to accept these things, but it was absolutely necessary for me to do so before I could truly get better. But now it works better for me to not give shots and having diabetes any more attention than I have to.

If I start feeling down in the dumps, I go out in my yard and watch critters or lay in the sun, get something to eat, hang out with Miri or Wayne, or tell myself I will feel better again and go sleep it off. Seeing how Wayne handles having diabetes also helps me keep in mind that I still have a lot of good in my life and that the low times will pass.

Sometimes I get caught in feeling sorry for myself, but that makes me feel worse. What helps me most is to think about what I can do right now that I would enjoy, and then to go and do it.

The deep bond of love I share with Miri and Wayne has helped me come through the difficult experiences I've had. I don't think I would have made it without their love and support in so many ways. I didn't fully recognize how important their love was to me until I lost Jase and became so very sick.

After Jase died, for a while it was harder for me to accept and take in others' love or to get very fully involved in living again. My body was affected, too; it was harder for me to digest and be nourished by the food I ate. Even after I began hunting again and was spending more time with Miri and Wayne, at first I didn't allow myself to be fully nourished by food or by love.

Miri and Wayne's love gradually got through to me during the many months they nursed me back to health. As they continued to care for me, I realized more strongly the depth and importance of the bond of love we share. I also came to clearly know that I wanted to continue living and sharing my love with them in whatever ways I still can.

It's like I had to get so sick I nearly died before I realized how important love is to me. Only then could I again connect back with life more fully, and allow love to support me through whatever else I have to face in my life.

What matters most of all to me now is knowing I am loved and being able to express my love to others and have it be received and appreciated. It also helps, of course, to have good food and a wonderful yard to enjoy. It was great to feel strong and in control of things like I used to, but I now know I'm loved and special even though I can't hunt and watch over the yard like I used to.

It's still important for me to do what I can for others, like being there for Miri and sharing about my life experiences if that can possibly help someone else.

Wayne's sharing about how he came to terms with having diabetes, his reminding me that I must have shots to feel good, and his example of giving himself shots without focusing on them any more than he needed to were all crucial in helping me accept having diabetes and getting shots. His sharing also helped me move beyond shots feeling like such a big deal to being able to enjoy life again.

I truly hope my sharing might be helpful to someone in the ways Wayne's sharing has helped, and still helps, me.

I don't fully understand how books work for you humans. Miri tells me that the marks she makes on paper with her pen or computer

Reflections

tell whoever looks at them what I've been sharing with her. Pictures make more sense to me, and I like the idea of having a picture of me on the front of my book. That's kind of cool! Miri also had me dip my paw in red food coloring and make a print of my paw on paper to put in my book. She says that's a way of my saying it's really by me.

Miri spends more time with me since we've been working together on my book. I really need that, and I'm glad she is finally taking the time to just be with me, listen to me, and hear me. I've wanted her to do that for a long, long, time. She so easily gets all caught up in the stuff she has to do and forgets to make the time to just be still with me. She needs that as much as I do.

It was hard for Miri to learn to slow down enough to be fully present with me and open to receiving what I had to share with her without thinking about, analyzing, or judging it. She was worried about what people would think about her if she not only talked to a cat, but also "heard" what a cat said back to her.

Miri would start to be able to hear me a little, and then she would question what she'd heard me say and shut down again. She couldn't quite believe that she really heard me, and was trying too hard to "do" it right. I don't fully understand why this was, and is sometimes still, so difficult for her to do.

I keep on telling Miri that all she really needs to do is to spend time regularly being fully present with me, be open to receiving whatever I share with her, believe it is truly possible for her to hear me, and then to accept and trust what she hears.

Even more important to me than sharing through my book has been the deeper communication and sharing with Miri that has become possible by our working in this way together. I deeply need for our sharing to continue for me to have a sense of purpose and meaning in my life now.

I still have a lot of love and understanding to share, even though I can't do many of the things I used to be able to do. And I need love and understanding, too! I think that I can help support and teach Miri how to open more deeply to other ways of knowing and understanding, if she wants to learn this. I need to not only feel loved and special, but also to be heard and accepted for who I am and what I have to share.

We cats, and other four-legged animals, feel, know and understand much more than you humans usually give us credit for. And we also love to share and to be heard and understood by others, just like you do, especially by those beings close to us.

If you truly want to hear us, all you need to do is believe this is possible for you, ask us with respect to share with you, slow down your mind, and be open to taking in whatever we share. We need to know that you really want to hear us, and that you consider our feelings and perspective important to know about, like you would with any friend.

Communication with us will take some practice, as with anything you are learning and aren't used to doing. The slowing down part seems especially difficult for you humans. But know that you truly can communicate with us, two-ways, if you believe you can, stick with practicing doing it, and trust what you hear.

There are several different ways you can receive from us without words, telepathically. Samantha picks up information visually, through her bodily senses, and also through pure thought. Miri takes in communications from me as a kind of global knowing about what I'm thinking and experiencing. Sometimes she gets pictures, feelings, or sensations, but mostly she just knows. She doesn't always get all the details right, but she's getting better.

You humans can also learn to communicate among yourselves in this way, as well as with cats and other animals. In order to communicate with another being without words, you both have to truly want to share honestly with each other. You can't lie when you are communicating telepathically. There must be trust, respect, and safety for this kind of exchange to happen.

You must also be willing to let go of trying to make things happen the way you want them to and think they should, and just be fully present with whatever is there and accept it as it is.

Reflections

Isn't that what we all most want from those we love? It's what matters more than anything else to me now.

Miri

Part B: MIRI'S STORY

Diana Living Through Life's Challenges

Diana and Miri

Chapter 9

LEARNING TO HEAR DIANA

"*Just go back and start doing it,*" I was told that day on the desert, long ago, when I'd questioned how I could possibly take on the task of writing down Diana's story.

"*The way to move ahead will open for you as you go back and spend more time with Diana, asking her questions and being open to hearing whatever she shares,*" my instruction continued.

I had to get started somewhere, ready or not, so I set aside some time each week to be with Diana and work on the task I had been given. I started spending regular time with Diana several months after the last session Diana, Jada, and I had with Samantha, after it had become clear that Samantha would not be able to work with Diana on her book.

As Diana had no difficulty understanding me when I was clear in what I sent her, I focused on my learning to better receive from her. Before I could begin to write a book, I needed to have material for a book, and before I could have material for a book, I needed to be able to hear Diana much more clearly.

The idea of our work together evolving into a book was too overwhelming and scary for me to think about, at first. I spent my initial time with Diana simply asking her about things she liked or wanted to share with me. I enjoyed learning to know her better, and she was glad I was spending more time with her and that I wanted to hear and understand her better.

Diana was almost always willing to share about anything positive whenever I slowed down and focused long enough to pick up from her. I was pleasantly surprised to be able to receive some information pretty clearly the first few times I tried, and most of the time for several months. Some of her early responses included:

(1) *"To know how loved I am"* (when asked what has helped her most through a difficult time);
(2) *"Being sick; it is really hard to not be able to count on my body, and to not know how I will feel at any time on any day"* (when asked what was most difficult for her);
(3) *"My left foot is tired and aching all the time";*
(4) *"Wayne explaining to me and showing me, and knowing he also has to take shots every day and that he feels well and strong most of the time"* (when asked what most helped her accept getting shots; and
(5) *"To focus on things they can do and enjoy doing...like for me, watching the birds and being in my yard helped me feel better"* (when asked what she'd most t\like to tell little kids to help them deal with having diabetes.

I was able to receive some information fairly regularly for several months whenever I made the time I needed to settle into an open and receptive space. But then, after sharing a couple of times with close friends who were genuinely interested, my ability to receive shut down, and for a while I couldn't pick up anything clearly, or felt like I was imagining it if I did.

It seemed like the harder I tried, the less I got, and the less I got, the harder I tried...and it became a vicious cycle, that I became very deeply stuck in.

Determined to learn to do this right, I reviewed my notes and tapes from Samantha. I concentrated my initial efforts on trying to pick up visual and sensory impressions, as Samantha teaches and does in her own work. Sometimes I received very fragmentary images or impressions, but more often I got nothing.

At first there seemed to be no rhyme or reason as to when it worked for me and when it didn't.

Over time it gradually became clear to me that receiving information visually and kinesthetically, as Samantha does, did not work very well for me. At first it hadn't occurred to me that there could be another way. I just became more and more discouraged as I tried to see and feel things. Even when I did get occasional fleeting glimpses or sensations, few came with any clarity or feeling of certainty that they were from Diana.

But then I began to notice, when I succeeded in slowing my usual mental chatter until I was very still and could let go of trying so hard, that I sometimes received strong clear flashes of knowing. These flashes were often about things I did not know before, was not thinking about, and did not feel like were coming from me. When I could allow this to happen, knowledge and information flowed easily into my awareness.

Gradually, over time, I recognized that the way I best take in information is different from Samantha's, though the basic approach and attitude are the same.

Samantha's teachings were essential to my having been able to come this far. She taught me the need for a strong desire to communicate with four-legged animals, as well as faith and belief that it is possible to do. Her teachings include the importance of having respect for the spirit of the animal you wish to share with, of asking for the animal's willingness to communicate with you, and of expecting that two-way communication will happen.

Samantha in her teachings also stresses the necessity for being clear in your intent and in the images and thoughts that you send. Having an attitude of allowing and of being open to whatever might happen, rather than trying to make something happen, is also basic to her approach.

All that I learned from Samantha provided a foundation upon which a way of receiving that worked for me was slowly able to develop. While I occasionally saw a picture or felt physical sensations, most of what I picked up that felt like it was truly from Diana came to me as a kind of global knowing that felt more basic than words. My task seemed to be one of consciously allowing this basic knowing to flow through me and then expressing it by way of words, as a translation of sorts.

Over time this sense of knowing came to feel to me like a basic language, or a kind of form or essence of knowing, that is behind the use of language and words as we usually think of them. It seemed to me like this knowing could potentially be expressed through any language, or without any. My impression was that if one tuned in to this basic kind of knowing, there would be no need for words as we're accustomed to thinking about and using them. And words fall very short of describing my sense of such knowing.

Sometimes I spent time just lying on the floor or in the yard next to Diana, with no focus on communication of information. At such times I just held her in my awareness. This was more of a sharing of energy than of information, and felt really good.

At other times I asked Diana questions, or asked if there was anything she wanted to share with me. Sometimes Diana responded, at other times she didn't (or, if she did, I didn't "hear" her). If she didn't want to share about what I'd asked her, she changed the subject. Occasionally she initiated telling me something spontaneously. She was usually glad to share when I came from a place of clear desire, intent, belief, and focus.

As Diana and I continued working together, I gradually began to identify some things that got in the way of my receiving clearly from her. Trying too hard, or getting frustrated with my slowness and ineptitude closed me down. When I was distracted by ordinary life stuff on my mind, Diana became upset and frustrated with me, and often didn't want to share with me for a while. And negative beliefs about what I was doing blocked any progress.

I had not realized how many negative judgmental messages I had buried in my psyche about doing this kind of work. Again and again I had to look deeply at why I wasn't picking up anything, and negative beliefs were often in the way.

Thoughts like "No one will believe you," "There's no scientific proof for this," "You're making this all up," continued to raise their ugly heads. Over and over I had to bring such negative beliefs to greater consciousness and actively replace them with affirmative thoughts that supported my moving ahead.

Whenever I started questioning or doubting what was coming through to me, the line of communication shut down and I would get nothing more, sometimes for days or even weeks. If I started wondering where this endeavor would take me, I became afraid of what might happen in the future, and that also totally shut me down. When I was emotionally distressed or tired, I received only very vague impressions, at best. And being in a rational, analytical mental space did not work at all.

My window was difficult to open and easily closed.

Even after I clearly realized how much my capacity to receive depended on my being in the right state of mind (or non-mind), my ability to get into and stay in a receptive, open, space was like a delicate fragile plant that needed careful protection and nurturing to further develop.

Almost any sharing with others closed the window of my ability to receive. Anyone else's skepticism, questioning, or even simple curiosity tapped into my uncertainty, which shut me down. After having two such experiences, I stopped sharing with anyone except very minimally with my husband and one close friend, until Diana and I completed the first draft of her part of the book.

For many months, it felt like the book was in danger of miscarriage because of the precariousness of my developing ability to hear Diana telepathically.

In order to stand a chance of taking in information clearly from Diana, I needed to have a block of time of at least several hours with no distractions. I used relaxation, meditation, and self-hypnosis to slow down my usual mind chatter and whole being until I was in a calm, centered, still place within myself.

As I was used to spending much of my time in a rational frame of mind, it took some practice not to be. Intuition provided a bridge for me, as intuitive awareness has been essential to my work as a psychologist for many years. An intuitive way of perceiving is closer to the kind of mental space I needed to be in to receive information from Diana, but not quite the same.

The mental space I was in when I felt I was truly picking up accurately from Diana seemed in some ways different from any I was used to. It required, as did intuitive awareness, slowing down my constant mental chatter that goes on so continually if I don't intentionally stop it.

It was also necessary to create a still, open, receptive space deep within myself from which to recognize and welcome whatever impressions and information came in.

In addition, it also required a very conscious focused awareness, like a tuning in to a very specific frequency…the frequency of Diana's mind. And there was that quality of clear knowing to the information I felt was definitely from Diana.

Frequently there was also an element of surprise for me when Diana shared something I'd had no idea about. I hadn't realized that she was afraid we wouldn't want her around anymore when she'd pooped all over the kitchen floor when in shock after the fox attacked and injured her. Or that many years later, she still didn't feel fully comfortable and safe in her beloved yard despite knowing I had taken the fox far away and securely covered the hole in the fence.

I had also not realized the profoundness of Diana's ecstatic enjoyment of eating freshly killed prey. Or that the quality of baby Jada's quick darting at her brought up memories of the way the fox had moved when he attacked and injured her.

Diana clearly knew that Jada was not the fox and could not injure her as the fox had done. But this didn't prevent her from reliving the terrifying experience she'd had with the fox whenever Jada's movement was similar to how the fox had moved when attacking her. Realizing that Diana was suffering from symptoms of post-traumatic stress disorder helped me better understand the extreme degree of difficulty Diana had accepting baby Jada at first.

I realize none of these things prove I received information accurately from Diana, or even that I received anything at all from her. I could have imagined everything. I only know that I have had to learn to trust what I receive when my heart feels it is valid.

Diana on her author's chair

Chapter 10

WORKING WITH DIANA ON HER BOOK

As Diana and I continued to meet together over time, the material she shared with me accumulated, flowing together with no form or structure, like a huge pool of cloudy water.

I felt overwhelmed whenever I thought of creating a book out of the amorphous collection of information. Where to begin? I felt like I was treading water with nothing to hold onto, nothing to guide me. I'd never written a book before, and I'd never listened in depth to a cat before, much as I've loved my feline companions.

While the content was from Diana, she left it totally up to me to arrange it into a book. She didn't really understand why we humans wrote things down, anyway. But she accepted that this was what I needed to do, in order to pass on what she told me to others who might be interested in and able to benefit from her sharing.

The actual times of interaction with Diana had become very heart-warming and good for me. I was again and again touched by her simple, honest, direct perspective on life, by the depth of her awareness and love, and by her courageous facing of the difficult challenges that came her way. But she could not help me with the task of organizing all the material she had shared with me.

In the midst of my floundering, I noticed an ad for a three-hour class offered through the Learning Annex on *How To Write A Book On Anything In Two Weeks Or Less.* A rather preposterous title, I thought.

While it seemed to me unrealistic and unlikely that I or anyone else could write a book in two weeks or less, I decided to attend the class anyway, hoping it might offer something that would help me develop a form for Diana's book. It did. During the exercises provided in the three hours of the class, I was able to imagine what the main chapters of the book should be. The class also provided useful guidelines that later helped me arrange information within the chapters and chapters within the book.

Having an organizational structure for the book also helped clarify areas of content that were missing or incomplete, where I needed to gather more information. Much of my interaction with Diana now became more like an interview process. We explored specific subjects in more depth, or clarified and expanded on information I already had about other topics.

Whenever I was going to communicate with Diana in any depth, I continued to need a block of time where I wouldn't be interrupted or distracted. I also always had to go through a process of letting go of anything else on my mind and of consciously slowing down mentally until I was in a still, centered, open place in myself. Only then could I tune in to Diana with any certainty that it was she I was hearing.

Occasionally I was able to shift gears and tune in to Diana easily and quickly. More often it took me an hour or more before I was able to connect with Diana deeply and strongly enough to receive from her clearly. Sometimes I did not succeed.

Diana was usually ready and wanting to share with me once I had stopped my usual mind chatter, brought my focus totally to her, and was open and ready to hear *whatever* she had to say. Sometimes she not only responded to my questions, but volunteered additional information. At other times she did not answer me or changed to another subject.

At first I wondered if Diana was bored when she changed the subject. She wouldn't reply when asked about this. There were several topics where Diana immediately changed the subject when asked what her feelings about them were. These included:

(1) Jason's death;
(2) Her own near-death experience from her diabetic crisis;
(3) The fox's attack and injury to her leg, and
(4) Jada coming to join our family.

These were all topics about which Diana had experienced significant distress and/or trauma.

Through probing gently and slowly working around the edges of these sensitive issues with Diana, it became obvious that she still had very distressing feelings about them all. While she had come to terms with these experiences at one level, part of her way of coping had been to bury some of the feelings that hurt too much.

I encouraged Diana to start sharing her feelings about these painful experiences with me, little by little, as she could. I assured her that it would help her feel better if she didn't hold her feelings in, but expressed them to me and had them be heard and accepted. I told her it would also help children and adult humans who were going through some of the same kind of things she'd been through to know about the feelings she'd had to deal with, and to find out whether it helped her to talk about them.

Gradually Diana began to tell me more about some of the initially overwhelming feelings and fears she'd had and struggled with. To do this, she had to go back in time and walk through the experiences again, so to speak. Most of her sharing about these central challenges in her life is therefore in the present tense.

Diana was eventually willing to respond to almost everything I asked her about, after we'd gone through the above process. There was one aspect of Jase's death, the fact that it was assisted, that neither one of us said very much about. I think it was too sensitive a topic for us both.

A number of times Diana shared spontaneously about something, far beyond any specific questions I'd asked her. This happened, for example, as she told me about the pleasures of hunting and the joys of being out in her yard. It also happened when I asked her about what she'd learned from all the challenging life experiences she's been through. Most of the content of her last chapter flowed out as a continuous stream of sharing over several hours, with almost no further questioning needed from me.

It was wonderful to see Diana blossom during our work together. She seemed more confident and self-assured in her whole demeanor. Physically, she came out of hiding away from Jada so much and was in the open and around us more. She also felt freer to go throughout the far corners of her beloved yard again, without fear of the fox reappearing.

Diana also began to stand up for herself more assertively with young Jada. She frequently sat on her special "author's chair" as we worked together, and did not allow Jada to go there. That was her special place and hers alone.

Jada, Diana and Miri working together

Working with Diana on Her Book

Jada initially became jealous of my focus on Diana during all the time Diana and I spent working together on the book. I explained to Jada that Diana was elderly and unwell and did not have many more years with us. I told Jada that she also would have an opportunity to share more, later, as she was young and healthy and would hopefully be with us for a long time to come.

Jada frequently sat nearby as Diana and I worked on the book, assisting us with her energy. She had a favorite spot where she liked to be as we worked together…curled in a low box beside me on the desk. She came to mostly accept being subordinate to Diana in relation to the book, and gave us what support she could.

I am deeply grateful for Diana's incredible patience with me, most of the time, as I fumblingly found my way. At times she became very frustrated with my slowness, by my allowing myself to be so easily distracted, and by my questioning or doubting what was happening. She often gently chided me, and at other times walked away in disgust and ignored me for a while.

But again and again she forgave me, and encouraged me to stick with it, telling me "*You can do it, Miri.*" She supported me in working through my numerous blocks and gently guided me along the steps I needed to take to keep on keeping on. I could not have had a more excellent, devoted, and loving teacher.

Diana Living Through Life's Challenges

Diana

Chapter 11

REMEMBERING DIANA
(1981-1998)

I will always remember the nearly seventeen years that Diana shared our lives in the form of a most beautiful calico cat. She indeed embodied the goddess of hunting, after whom she was named. Deeply connected to nature, independent, huntress par excellence, she was queen of the wilderness of our backyard.

Diana's black, white, and golden body was crowned by a most unusual, asymmetrical, gold and black face with sea-green eyes that flashed like brilliant emeralds when the light caught them. Her soul and spirit as beautiful as her body, she gave love and acceptance freely to all those beings dear to her.

I first saw Diana's unique, tiny face and her intense eyes peering out at me from a cage in the front office of a cat shelter where I was searching for a beloved feline friend, Little One, who had suddenly disappeared. I wasn't feeling ready or wanting to get another cat companion at the time. But Little One had been gone for several months, and I'd decided this would have to be my last trip to the shelter looking for her.

Diana Living Through Life's Challenges

My eyes were held by Diana's captivating gaze through the bars of the cage for new arrivals in the shelter office. The manager noticed the two of us staring at each other and, despite my feeble protestations, got her out and handed her to me. She settled right down purring contentedly. Totally enchanted, I took her along home with me after she fell asleep on my lap.

What a tease baby Diana was! And how proud she was when she was finally able to jump up onto the kitchen counter and go outside on her own through the cat "door" in the window. Near the end of her life, Diana's pride in getting outside on her own again showed itself when, sick, weak, and hardly able to walk, she recovered enough to take herself out through the cat door. She was sitting there, waiting for me to find and see her, when I got home!

Best Friends

The deep love Diana and Jason shared was touching to observe. They usually slept and napped with their bodies touching or intertwined in some way.

During Jason's last days of serious illness, Diana stayed faithfully by his side, giving what comfort and support she could. Losing Jason was extremely traumatic for Diana, and she went into a severe depression following his death.

Remembering Diana

Longing for Jason's loving presence back and thinking she would have this again in baby Jada, how disappointed Diana was that Jada didn't look or act like Jase when she arrived. Already elderly and often not feeling well, it was very difficult for Diana to cope with Jada's high level of energy. But over time, she came to accept and love Jada, and could eventually see Jase's spirit in her.

Diana brought me gifts of whatever she found that she liked or thought I might like or be able to use. She appreciated beautiful and unusual things, and her gifts included many varieties of leaves and pieces of wood in addition to too numerous prey, pieces of left over food, cigarettes, a metal tape measure, and small sand shovel (I had a sandbox in which I played). She had a special "present call" announcing when she was bringing me something.

I'll always treasure an arrangement I made of some of Diana's gifts of leaves and wood as well as the tape measure, which must have been difficult for her to carry.

Our backyard was clearly Diana's domain, and she loved it dearly and watched over it well. She kept the rats and mice under control in the bushes, woodpiles, and sheds. She protected the yard behind our house and challenged any other four-legged animals who dared enter…even the fox.

It was awesome to observe Diana's rapt attention while stalking her prey. Her ever watchful, perceptive awareness noticed everything. She could move with such stealth and quietness of both mind and body that neither we nor the critters she was pursuing noticed her being nearby, though the white flag at the end of her tail often gave away her proximity to us.

At times, my experience of Diana's presence was so strong it was almost palpable. She had such a noble aura of wisdom, love and awareness that it was special for me to just be close to her.

Diana was always nearby with comforting energy if I was worried or sick She took on whatever she could of my stress and unresolved feelings, trying to relieve me of them. She allowed me to hold and hug her tightly because she knew how much it meant to me, even though she didn't like it all that much. She continued being there for me as best she could, until she could no more.

On the other hand, Diana would at times be incredibly stubborn when she'd made up her mind about something, like her human mom. She didn't like it when we were away from home for more than a day or two, and often ignored us for days upon our return. And if she decided she didn't want a shot, I had to wait until she was hungry enough to accept it.

Much as she hated change, Diana continued to face and deal with the many adjustments she had to make when she became ill, was injured, and had a new baby sibling to put up with. She even accepted being more dependent on us and having to get shots and pills in order to stay here with us as long as she could.

Diana wanted to continue to share her love with us as long as she knew she was loved and special, and as long as she could still enjoy life and contribute to others in some way. She was one of the most gentle, accepting and loving beings I have ever known. Diana supported me in whatever ways she could, both during her life and after her death. Her love for me was more unconditional than any other I have ever known.

Diana was so grateful and happy when I started spending more time with her and could finally begin to hear her better. It was a joy to me to see her regain more sense of meaning, purpose and happiness as we worked together on her book.

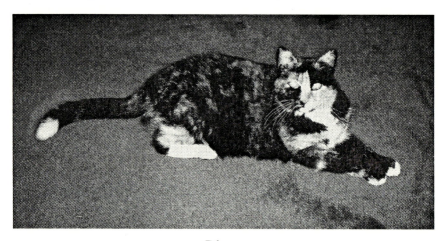

Diana

Again and again Diana put up with my recurring doubt, distractibility, and slowness, continuing to believe in me. When I slacked off more than she thought was acceptable, she chided me. At times she became discouraged, impatient, and even disgusted with me, but always ended up giving me more chances, even when I'd failed and disappointed her really badly.

Diana kept challenging me to further development of my awareness. "*You can do it, Miri*," she constantly reassured me, always encouraging me to keep doing the best I could. Repeatedly she reminded me of the importance of taking good care of myself and of making time regularly to be still, in order to help me move ahead on my path and deepen my connection with Spirit and with her, my teacher. I am deeply grateful for her patience, love and acceptance, as well as for her blunt direct honesty.

Diana had a wonderful sense of humor and loved to play. Up until almost the end of her life, she continued to create little games to play with us, like trying to beat Wayne to his chair (Diana also described playing this game with Wayne in Chapter 4).

When Diana knew Wayne and I were about to have dinner, she jumped up onto his chair and quickly made herself appear to be comfortable, pretending not to realize that he was about to sit on the chair. Or, if she was already eating her own food and Wayne got to his chair first, she would lay in wait nearby. Then, if he got up to get something, she would jump onto his chair and look at us innocently. In either case, we would laugh and move Wayne's chair, with her on it, between us, and Wayne would get himself another chair.

Another special memory is of Diana claiming her favorite place under the Christmas tree from a little train. On Diana's last Christmas with us, we'd put up a small train encircling our Christmas tree. In the evening, though very weak and ill, she came out to join us in the living room.

Fascinated by the movement of the train, Diana went over to the track and started following the train as it moved to the left around the back of the tree. She then backed up as it came around towards her

Diana Living Through Life's Challenges

from the right, again started after it as it moved away and backed up again as it came around from the right, and etc.

When we finally stopped the train it was behind the tree, and Diana went back to check it out. She smelled and looked at it carefully, and then proceeded to push the train off the track and lie down on top of it, claiming her right to her favorite spot under the tree!

On her last day with us in bodily form, Diana was too weak to walk anymore. It was a warm day for the first of February. I carried her out into the yard in her favorite box from the back porch, the box she loved to lie in and watch over her yard from.

Lying on the earth her last day with us

Diana wanted me to put her directly on the earth. I didn't think that was a good idea because of how cool the earth was and how low her body temperature had gone. I explained that to her as best I could, but she didn't agree with me.

Determined, as usual, Diana managed to get herself out of the box and right on the earth where she wanted to be.

Remembering Diana

Diana left her body around 5:00 a.m. on February 2nd, 1998. I had the privilege of holding her during the last hours of her life and of witnessing her courageous leap out of her body across the chasm into another reality where I could not follow.

As I wept the tears I'd held in for weeks over the lifeless form that no longer contained her spirit, Diana reminded me that she was not in her body anymore. She gently but emphatically pointed out that I needed to let go of her physical body and relate to her now as a spiritual being.

Shortly after Diana's death, I again went out to the desert to spend some time alone grieving and healing. At one point I felt drawn to go to a favorite spot by an oasis in a palm grove. As I prayed and meditated by the oasis, I asked Diana for some sign that she truly lived on.

It was a calm, sunny day, but suddenly a strong wind whipped fiercely around the tops of the palm trees. I had a vision of Diana dancing freely in the midst of the wind and flowing palm fronds, and these words came clearly to me:

> *I will always love you, Miri, and I will always be there for*
> *You when you take the time to stop and slow down your*
> *Mind enough to know this.*

As quickly as it had come, the wind was gone again, and I was filled with deep peace and reassurance.

And then, just as clearly, the following words of my heart's response to Diana came to me:

At the oasis

Remembering Diana

Goodby, beautiful Diana,

Your black, white, golden Calico form
    No longer graces us with watchful presence;
The warm comfort of your furry body next to mine
    Will be no more;
Your green mysterious jeweled eyes
    No longer flash or gaze with love.

I miss you as I've known you,
    Beloved friend, companion, healer, huntress.
I saw the deep sadness in your eyes
    When you said you could not stay.

Thank you for dancing for me in the wind, in the palms,
    By the oasis, source of life.
Thank you for telling me you will always love me,
    Always be there when I need you, and am ready.

The winter of my grief
    Has long been dark,
But spring returns with new green growth
    Bursting forth from barren branches.

Your illness took us to Samantha,
    Who opened my heart
To greater knowing and sharing with you,
    Forever.

Because I love you, I am glad you now are free
    To run again, to dance, to fly!
You stayed with me until you could no more.
    My heart pain feels your joy and is renewed.
I will always love you, beautiful Diana.
    I thank you for your love.

Bodi el Tigre

Epilogue
LIFE CONTINUES TO UNFOLD

Diana and I had two and one-half more years together after we completed the first draft of her book in the summer of 1996. I wish I could say that my ability to hear Diana and Jada continued to deepen and improve all throughout that time and since.

In the fall of 1996, I enrolled in a creative non-fiction writing class, intending to fine-tune my writing skills so I could better revise the material for the book. I did, in fact, work further on the book before Diana's health took a turn for the worse in the summer of 1997, with her kidneys failing in October of that year.

Caring for Diana's health needs and spending time simply being and sharing with her then took priority over working more on the book until her transition out of her body in February, 1998, as well as for some time following her death.

During the last months of Diana's life we were blessed with the help and support of Anne Smith, V.M.D. It is thanks to Dr. Smith's excellent medical care that Diana survived her initial kidney failure, and we were able to have another six months together.

We were also greatly helped during this time by the support and insight of Sue Goodrich, a professional animal consultant Diana, Jada and I spoke with a number of times after Samantha had become ill and no longer came to the San Diego area.

At some point in the spring or summer of 1998, I joined a writing group that had been recommended by one of the women in the creative non-fiction writing class. After my third meeting with this writing group, I was asked not to return because one of the women in the group was a fundamental Christian and had trouble with the content of my writing.

Rejection by the writing group tapped deeply into many insecurities and fears I'd not fully dealt with, many of which went back to my own fundamental Christian upbringing. My fledgling ability to hear my animal companions mostly shut down, and work on Diana's book was shelved indefinitely.

Not until the spring of 2001 did I finally resume the task of deepening my ability to communicate with my animal companions and completing Diana's book and putting it out in the world. I made a commitment early in 2001 to do whatever I needed to do to move beyond my blocks and complete the book within this year.

I attended an advanced workshop with Penelope Smith, a leading professional interspecies communicator, which helped me face my fears and begin to hear four-legged animals more clearly again. The fine intuitive hypnotic work of Stephen Gilligan also greatly helped me clear out remnants of old issues and move into an expanded awareness of myself and of my connection with life.

Around the time of my birthday in the Spring of 2001, I took off several weeks, spending some of the time in the desert and some of it reconnecting again with the material of Diana's book and beginning to work further with it.

In the meantime, I am deeply grateful to all the powers helping me that I picked up on Diana's return. Diana had told me that she would return sometime in the year 2000, and that I would feel her in my body and thus know it was she. I was not in very much or very good contact with Diana's spirit, with Jada (our cat companion), or myself

Epilogue

at the time, on January 2nd, 2000, when I was rushing into a pet shop to buy food for Jada.

As I was leaving the pet store, a kitten meowed loudly, and I felt the energy of the cry run through my body like an electrical current. I was not thinking about Diana at the time or expecting her to return so soon, but I could not ignore what I'd just experienced. After spending time with the kittens, I believed Diana's spirit was in one of them, and brought him home to join our family.

Diana is now back with us in the form of a young energetic male cat, Bodi el Tigre. A wonderful blend of loving and athletic, Bodi enjoys testing the limits of his body, and seems to be trying to set new speed and agility records in running and climbing trees.

Working on the book with Bodi's support

Bodi has been very supportive of my completing the book and getting it out in the world, as has Jada. Having the same highly tuned spiritual energy, stubborn independence, high spirits and deeply loving essence as when he was here as Diana, Bodi continues to challenge me to move ahead in my inner growth and spiritual awareness. It is a blessing to have him/her back in my life.

MAJOR EVENTS IN DIANA'S LIFE

07/07/81 – Diana's birthday (estimate)

08/20/81 – Miri took Diana home from *Friends of Cats*

12/29/85 – Move to live with Wayne

01/08/90 – First meeting with Samantha Khury

09/26/90 – First meeting with Dr. Stephen Blake

06/24/92 – Jason's death

03/24/93 – Diabetic crisis

June/93 – Started hunting again

01/19/94 – Attacked by stranger

10/25/94 – Jada arrives

11/21/94 – Began work on book

10/11/95 – First meeting with Sue Goodrich

August/96 – First draft of book completed

06/28/97 – First meeting with Dr. Anne Smith

10/04/97 – Kidney failure

02/02/98 – Diana's transition out of bodily form

RELATED READING

Adams, Janine. *You Can Talk To Your Animals.* IDG Books, 2000.

Anderson, Allen (Editor) & Anderson, Linda (Editor). *Angel Animals: Exploring Our Spiritual Connection With Animals.* Plume, 1999.

Andrews, Ted. *Animal Speak.* Llewellyn Publications, 1993.

Bardens, Dennis. *Psychic Animals.* Henry Holt & Co., 1987.

Bennett, Hal Zena. *Spirit Animals and the Wheel of Life.* Hampton Roads Publishing Co., 2001.

Boone, J. Allen. *Adventures in Kinship With All Life.* Tree of Life, 1990.

Boone, J. Allen. *Kinship With All Life.* Harper & Row, 1954; Harper Collins, 1976.

Brunke, Dawn Bauman. *Animal Voices: Telepathic Communication in the Web of Life.* Inner Traditions Intl. Ltd., 2002.

Church, Julie Adams. *Uncommon Friends: Celebrating the Human-Animal Bond.* H. J. Kramer, 2002.

Diedrich, Monica. *What Your Animals Tell Me: Through True Stories, An Animal Communicator Reveals the Fascinating and Heart-Warming Inner World of Our Pets.* Two Paws Press, 2001.

Fate Magazine. *Psychic Pets and Spirit Animals.* Gramercy, 2000.

Fitzpatrick, Sonya. *What The Animals Tell Me.* Hyperion, 1997.

Graham, Bernie. *Creature Comfort: Animals That Heal.* Prometheus Books, 2000.

Gurney, Carol. *The Language of Animals: 7 Steps To Communicating With Animals.* Dell Books (Paperbacks), 2001.

Herriot, James. *All Creatures Great and Small.* St. Martins Press, 1972.

Hiby, Lydia with Weintraub, Bonnie S. *Conversations With Animals.* New Sage Press, 1998.

Hobe, Phyllis (Ed.). *Listening To the Animals.* A series of books of true stories of human-animal relationships. Guideposts, 2001-2002.

Kinkade, Amelia. *Straight From the Horse's Mouth: How to Talk to Animals and Get Answers.* Crown Publishers, 2001.

Kolb, Janice Gray. *Journal of Love: Spiritual Communication With Animals Through Journal Writing.* Blue Dolfin Publ., 2000.

Laland, Stephanie. *Animal Angels.* Guideposts, 1998.

Laland, Stephanie & Day, Doris. *Peaceful Kingdom: Random Acts of Kindness by Animals.* Conari Press, 1997.

Lydecker, Beatrice. *What The Animals Tell Me.* Harper & Row, 1977.

Lydecker, Beatrice. *Stories the Animals Tell Me.* Harper & Row, 1978.

McElroy, Susan Chernak. *Animals as Teachers and Healers.* New Sage Press, 1996; Ballantine, 1997.

Meyer, Judy. *The Animal Connection: A Guide to Intuitive Communication With Your Pet.* Plume, 2000.

Morrison, Barbara. *I Talk to the Animals.* Barbara Morrison, 2001.

Moussaieff Masson, Jeffrey. *Dogs Never Lie About Love.* Crown Publishers, Inc., 1997.

Moussaieff Masson, Jeffrey & McCarthy, Susan. *When Elephants Weep.* Delacorte Press, 1995.

Myers, Arthur. *Communicating With Animals: The Spiritual Connection Between People and Animals.* Contemporary Books, 1997.

Newhouse, Flower A. *These, Too, Shall Be Loved.* The Christward Ministry, 1976.

Noel, Brigitte. *The Silent Conversation: Telepathy With Companion Animals.* wwwBrigitteNoel.com, 2002

Palmer, Jessica Dawn. *Animal Wisdom.* Thorsons Publishers, 2001.

Pitcairn, Richard H. & Pitcairn, Susan Hubble. *Dr. Pitcairn's Complete Guide to Natural Health for Dogs and Cats.* Rodale Press, 1982.

Pope, Raphaela & Morrison, Elizabeth. *Wisdom of the Animals: Communication Between Animals and the People Who Love Them.* Adams Media Corporation, 2001.

Randour, Mary Lou & McElroy, Susan Chernak. *Animal Grace: Entering a Spiritual Relationship With Our Fellow Creatures.* New World Library, 2000.

Roads, Michael J. *Journey Into Nature.* H. J. Kramer, Inc., 1990.

Roads, Michael J. *Journey Into Oneness.* H. J. Kramer, Inc., 1994.

Roads, Michael J. *Talking With Nature.* H. J. Kramer, Inc., 1985, 1987.

Schoen, Allen. *Love, Miracles, and Animal Healing.* Simon & Schuster, 1995.

Sheldrake, Rupert. *Dogs That Know When Their Owners Are Coming Home.* Crown Publishing, 1999.

Smith, Penelope. *Animal Talk.* Beyond Words Publishing, Inc., 1999

Smith, Penelope. *Animals: Our Return To Wholeness.* Pegasus Publications, 1993.

Smith, Penelope. *When Animals Speak: Advanced Interspecies Communication.* Publisher's Group West, 1999.

Solisti-Mattelon, Kate. *Conversations With Cat: An Uncommon Catalog of Feline Wisdom.* Beyond Words Publishing Co., 2001.

Solisti-Mattelon, Kate. *Conversations With Dog: An Uncommon Dogalog of Canine Wisdom.* Beyond Words Publishing, 2000.

Solisti-Mattelon, Kate, Mattelon, Patrice, & Silver, Robert. *The Holistic Animal Handbook: A Guidebook to Nutrition, Health, and Communication.* Beyond Words Publishing, 2000.

Summers, Patty. *Talking With The Animals.* Hampton Roads, 1998.

Thomas, Elizabeth Marshall. *The Hidden Life of Dogs.* Houghton Mifflin Co., 1993.

Von Kreisler, Kristin. *The Compassion of Animals: True Stories of Animal Courage and Kindness.* Prima Publishing, 1997, 1999.

Webster, Richard. *Is Your Pet Psychic: Developing Psychic Communication With Your Pet.* Llewellyn Publications, 2002.

ABOUT THE AUTHORS

DIANA (1981-1998) was a wise, beautiful, and stubborn calico cat. Orphaned at a very young age, she was taken to *Friends of Cats*, where Miri met and adopted her. An excellent huntress and devoted friend to her beloved cat companion, Jason, and to her humans, Miri and Wayne, Diana came to pretty much take the goodness of her life for granted until her friend Jason died.

After losing Jason, Diana became deeply depressed and nearly died herself from a health crisis the following year. With much time on her paws as she was recovering, Diana grappled deeply with issues of meaning and purpose in living.

Diana helped teach Miri to hear her telepathically as she shared her story for this book. Most of the content of Diana's story was communicated when she was 15 and 16 years of age.

MIRI is Diana's human companion. She initially learned about telepathic communication with animals through seeing Samantha Khury, a professional interspecies communicator, work with Diana and Jason.

Miri's fledgling ability to telepathically communicate with and listen to an animal evolved during her work with Diana on this book. Although Miri also learned from a number of other interspecies communicators including Penelope Smith, Sue Goodrich, and Brigitte Noel, Diana was her primary teacher. Miri feels her work with Diana was an expansion and deepening of listening skills she had already developed and used as a psychologist.

Miri can be reached at: miria@mymailstation.com
acatstory.com

About the Book and Diana:

People and animals. People are lucky to have animals. I am not so sure the reverse is true. But since we are lucky to have critters in our lives, I think it is especially remarkable when people can acknowledge and explore the dimension of connection within the relationship they have with a special creature.

Some people have lots of animals...and they all have lessons to teach. However, it is the special individual that can tap into the fiber of our lives, help us see...and sort out issues that repeatedly trouble (us). Each species contributes dimension in their special way. Cats, charismatic, enigmatic, can be as personal or as detached as we allow.

Diana interfaced and wove her web into the fabric of Miri's life. Her message to Miri is as deep as life itself. Her effect on Miri will last her life and beyond. Diana's agenda is Miri's truth. Here is their story.

S. Anne Smith, V.M.D.
Holostic Veterinarian

My friendship with Diana was truly a gift. She gave information so graciously about her family and how she felt regarding her health and the many changes she had to accept... Through your stories about Diana's love, courage, and grace we will all be uplifted by her soul and essence. (Excerpt from letter to Miri)

Samantha Khury
Interspecies Communicator

If you are looking for a way to deepen your connection with your animal companion, read this book. After reading Diana and Miri's story, I know it is possible to communicate more clearly with other species.

I find what Diana shares, especially her last chapter, incredibly valuable...like a treatise on how to live. The relationship between Diana and

Miri is a wonderful example of a loving relationship in which Miri learns to be open, accepting and present with Diana as Diana is with her. Reading the book brings me back to a calm, peaceful sacred space.

Mel Karmen, Ph.D.
Psychotherapist

Diana's story reminds us again of the great web and circle of life and of the beautiful simplicity and power of love. I love the story. I read it in one sitting and wanted to keep reading some more. I met Diana, Miri and Jada/Jason when Diana was 15 years old. It's been a delight to be a part of their lives and see all three of them fulfill their abilities and promise.

Sue Goodrich
Animal Consultant

I knew as soon as I met (Diana) that she was a very old soul, who had come to teach her parents and me more about the eternal journey of life. She was a very beautiful feline with soulful eyes… She had many physical and emotional challenges on her journey and through it all she chose to move forward as a student and teacher… She was a little lioness in a cat suit (who) did not know…giving up… She will always have a special place in my heart… Her lesson to me was "Do your best and don't take it personally."

Stephen Blake, D.V.M.
ThePetWhisperer.com

This is an incredible story, beautifully told by both (Miri) and Diana. I was emotionally touched by Diana's experience of Jason's death, her fear of the (stranger), the loss of her security in the yard. It is an important story that needs to be shared. I would recommend that children and adults read it together.

Kathleen Estabrook
Holistic Health Practitioner